Scott Foresman - Addison Wesley

Virginia Math Connections

A Review and Practice Workbook

Project Coordinator
Debbie Owens

Contributing Writers
We wish to thank the following Virginia teachers:
Betsy Barton
Phoebe Clarke
Jill Davis
Sandra Dietz
Penny M. Gilliland
Edward Hockenberry
Kelley J. Miller
J. Diane Stanton
Candace S. Young

Scott Foresman - Addison Wesley

Editorial Offices: Glenview, Illinois • New York, New York
Sales Offices: Reading, Massachusetts • Duluth, Georgia • Glenview, Illinois
Carrollton, Texas • Menlo Park, California

http://www.sf.aw.com

Overview

Virginia Math Connections: A Review and Practice Workbook consists of these four sections of material.

Review worksheets provide practice of key skills and concepts that were covered last year in math class.

Virginia Connections worksheets provide interesting applications, problem sets, and puzzles dealing with themes and historical events related to the state of Virginia. There is one worksheet for each section of the Student Edition. Each worksheet applies and reinforces mathematical content from that section.

Practice worksheets provide additional practice on the concepts taught in each core lesson. For Learn and Explore lessons, the worksheets provide additional exercises that reflect those in the Connect section and/or the Skills and Reasoning section of the Student Edition Practice sets. For Problem Solving lessons, the worksheets closely mirror the Practice exercises in the Student Edition. Practice worksheets also include Section Reviews that supplement the Section Review pages in the Student Edition. Cumulative Review worksheets are included at the end of each chapter.

Chapter Tests Form A provide practice tests to help students prepare for chapter tests. Feedback from these practice tests can be used by students to assess their knowledge of the material taught in each chapter. Each Form A test covers all of the objectives of the chapter in the Student Edition in a free-response format.

Photo Credits

Photographs in this series courtesy of Virginia Tourism Corp., AP/Wide World Photos, UPI/Corbis-Bettmen, Visuals Unlimited, Library of Congress, International Harvester, The University of Virginia, Richmond Times Dispatch, The Richmond Kickers, Norfolk Zoological Park, Historic Crab Orchard Museum, The Claude Moore Colonial Farm, NASA, The British Museum.

ISBN 0-201-44843-2
Copyright © Addison Wesley Longman, Inc.

All rights reserved. No part of this publication may be reproduced, stored in a retrieval system, transmitted in any form or by any means, electronic, mechanical, photocopying, recording, or otherwise, without the prior written permission of the publisher.

Printed in the United States of America

5 6 7 8 9 10 - PO - 03 02 01 00

Contents

Review		1–2
Virginia Connections		
Virginia Connections	1A	1
Virginia Connections	1B	2
Virginia Connections	2A	3
Virginia Connections	2B	4
Virginia Connections	2C	5
Virginia Connections	3A	6
Virginia Connections	3B	7
Virginia Connections	3C	8
Virginia Connections	4A	9
Virginia Connections	4B	10
Virginia Connections	4C	11
Virginia Connections	5A	12
Virginia Connections	5B	13
Virginia Connections	6A	14
Virginia Connections	6B	15
Virginia Connections	7A	16
Virginia Connections	7B	17
Virginia Connections	7C	18
Virginia Connections	8A	19
Virginia Connections	8B	20
Virginia Connections	9A	21
Virginia Connections	9B	22
Virginia Connections	9C	23
Virginia Connections	10A	24
Virginia Connections	10B	25
Virginia Connections	10C	26
Virginia Connections	11A	27
Virginia Connections	11B	28
Virginia Connections	12A	29
Virginia Connections	12B	30

Practice

Chapter 1: Data, Graphs, and Facts Review

Practice	1-1	1
Practice	1-2	2
Practice	1-3	3
Practice	1-4	4
Practice	1-5	5
Practice	1-6	6
Section A *Review and Practice*		7
Practice	1-7	8
Practice	1-8	9
Practice	1-9	10
Practice	1-10	11
Practice	1-11	12
Section B *Review and Practice*		13
Cumulative Review Chapter 1		14

Chapter 2: Place Value and Time

Practice	2-1	15
Practice	2-2	16
Practice	2-3	17

Practice	2-4	18
Practice	2-5	19
Section A *Review and Practice*		20
Practice	2-6	21
Practice	2-7	22
Practice	2-8	23
Practice	2-9	24
Section B *Review and Practice*		25
Practice	2-10	26
Practice	2-11	27
Practice	2-12	28
Practice	2-13	29
Practice	2-14	30
Practice	2-15	31
Section C *Review and Practice*		32
Cumulative Review Chapter 2		33

Chapter 3: Adding Whole Numbers and Money

Practice	3-1	34
Practice	3-2	35
Practice	3-3	36
Practice	3-4	37
Section A *Review and Practice*		38
Practice	3-5	39
Practice	3-6	40
Practice	3-7	41
Practice	3-8	42
Practice	3-9	43
Practice	3-10	44
Section B *Review and Practice*		45
Practice	3-11	46
Practice	3-12	47
Practice	3-13	48
Practice	3-14	49
Practice	3-15	50
Practice	3-16	51
Practice	3-17	52
Section C *Review and Practice*		53
Cumulative Review Chapter 3		54

Chapter 4: Subtracting Whole Numbers and Money

Practice	4-1	55
Practice	4-2	56
Practice	4-3	57
Practice	4-4	58
Practice	4-5	59
Section A *Review and Practice*		60
Practice	4-6	61
Practice	4-7	62
Practice	4-8	63
Practice	4-9	64
Practice	4-10	65
Practice	4-11	66

Section B *Review and Practice*		67
Practice	4-12	68
Practice	4-13	69
Practice	4-14	70
Practice	4-15	71
Practice	4-16	72
Section C *Review and Practice*		73
Cumulative Review Chapter 4		74

Chapter 5: Multiplication Concepts and Facts

Practice	5-1	75
Practice	5-2	76
Practice	5-3	77
Section A *Review and Practice*		78
Practice	5-4	79
Practice	5-5	80
Practice	5-6	81
Practice	5-7	82
Practice	5-8	83
Practice	5-9	84
Practice	5-10	85
Section B *Review and Practice*		86
Cumulative Review Chapter 5		87

Chapter 6: More Multiplication Facts

Practice	6-1	88
Practice	6-2	89
Practice	6-3	90
Practice	6-4	91
Practice	6-5	92
Section A *Review and Practice*		93
Practice	6-6	94
Practice	6-7	95
Practice	6-8	96
Practice	6-9	97
Section B *Review and Practice*		98
Cumulative Review Chapter 6		99

Chapter 7: Division Concepts and Facts

Practice	7-1	100
Practice	7-2	101
Practice	7-3	102
Section A *Review and Practice*		103
Practice	7-4	104
Practice	7-5	105
Practice	7-6	106
Practice	7-7	107
Practice	7-8	108
Practice	7-9	109
Section B *Review and Practice*		110
Practice	7-10	111
Practice	7-11	112
Practice	7-12	113
Practice	7-13	114
Practice	7-14	115

Section C *Review and Practice*		116
Cumulative Review Chapter 7		117

Chapter 8: Using Geometry

Practice	8-1	118
Practice	8-2	119
Practice	8-3	120
Practice	8-4	121
Practice	8-5	122
Practice	8-6	123
Practice	8-7	124
Section A *Review and Practice*		125
Practice	8-8	126
Practice	8-9	127
Practice	8-10	128
Practice	8-11	129
Practice	8-12	130
Section B *Review and Practice*		131
Cumulative Review Chapter 8		132

Chapter 9: Multiplying and Dividing

Practice	9-1	133
Practice	9-2	134
Practice	9-3	135
Practice	9-4	136
Section A *Review and Practice*		137
Practice	9-5	138
Practice	9-6	139
Practice	9-7	140
Practice	9-8	141
Practice	9-9	142
Practice	9-10	143
Section B *Review and Practice*		144
Practice	9-11	145
Practice	9-12	146
Practice	9-13	147
Practice	9-14	148
Practice	9-15	149
Section C *Review and Practice*		150
Cumulative Review Chapter 9		151

Chapter 10: Fractions and Customary Linear Measurement

Practice	10-1	152
Practice	10-3	153
Practice	10-2	154
Practice	10-4	155
Practice	10-5	156
Section A *Review and Practice*		157
Practice	10-6	158
Practice	10-7	159
Practice	10-8	160
Practice	10-9	161
Practice	10-10	162
Section B *Review and Practice*		163
Practice	10-11	164
Practice	10-12	165
Practice	10-13	166
Practice	10-14	167
Practice	10-15	168
Section C *Review and Practice*		169
Cumulative Review Chapter 10		170

Chapter 11: Decimals and Metric Linear Measurement

Practice	11-1	171
Practice	11-2	172
Practice	11-3	173
Practice	11-4	174
Practice	11-5	175
Section A *Review and Practice*		176
Practice	11-6	177
Practice	11-7	178
Practice	11-8	179
Section B *Review and Practice*		180
Cumulative Review Chapter 11		181

Chapter 12: Measurement and Probability

Practice	12-1	182
Practice	12-2	183
Practice	12-3	184
Practice	12-4	185
Practice	12-5	186
Practice	12-6	187
Section A *Review and Practice*		188
Practice	12-7	189
Practice	12-8	190
Practice	12-9	191
Practice	12-10	192
Practice	12-11	193
Section B *Review and Practice*		194
Cumulative Review Chapter 12		195

Chapter Tests Form A

Chapter	1	1
Chapter	2	3
Chapter	3	5
Chapter	4	7
Chapter	5	9
Chapter	6	11
Chapter	7	13
Chapter	8	15
Chapter	9	17
Chapter	10	19
Chapter	11	21
Chapter	12	23

Virginia SOL Lessons

Related Facts: Addition and Subtraction	1
Related Facts: Multiplication and Division	2
Create and Solve Problems Involving Multiplication	3

Name _____

Review

Review From Last Year

1. Subtract.
Write the number sentence.

9 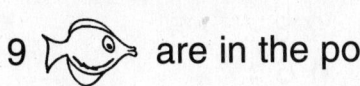 are in the pond.

5 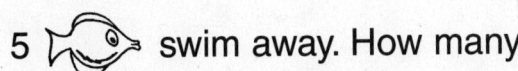 swim away. How many

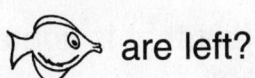 are left?

___ − ___ = ___

2. Write the rule.
Then write the missing number.

12	7
8	3
7	

3. Write the number.

3 tens   6 ones

_____

4. Write the numbers in order from least to greatest.

44 63 18   ___ ___ ___

5. Count the money.
Write the total amount.

_____ ¢

6. Write the time shown on the clock.

___ : ___

7. Add. Regroup if you need to.

   3 2 8
+ 1 4 6
———

8. Subtract. Regroup if you need to.

   6 5
− 1 9
———

Review 1

Name _____

Review

9. Write the numbers in order from greatest to least.

168, 92, 234, 351

_____, _____, _____, _____

10. Subtract. Regroup if you need to.

  7 8 ¢
− 1 6 ¢

11. How many centimeters long is the crayon?

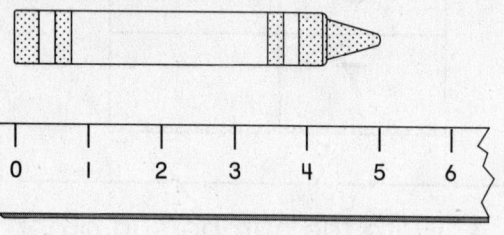

about _____ centimeters

12. Circle the object that is lighter than 1 kilogram.

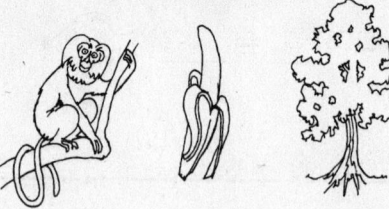

13. Use the solid figure. Write how many faces, corners, and edges.

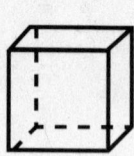

Faces _____

Corners _____

Edges _____

14. How was this shape moved? Write **slide**, **flip**, or **turn**.

15. What fraction of the bridges are covered?

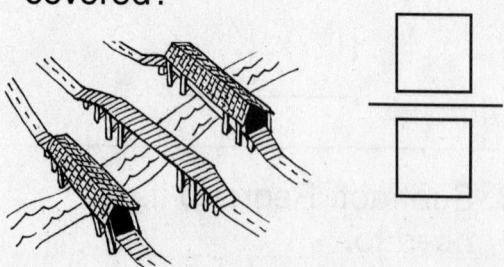

16. How many shoes? 8 groups of 2

_____ × _____ = _____ shoes

Name _____

Virginia
1A

Virginia Crops

While driving through the farming areas of Virginia, you will see many different crops. Some of these valuable crops are soybeans, corn, peanuts, potatoes, wheat, and apples.

Mr. Yoder farms 100 acres in Virginia. He grows corn, soybeans, wheat, and peanuts. Use the graph to answer each question.

Corn field

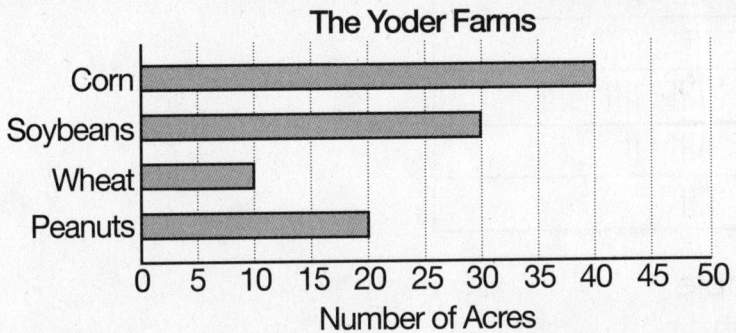

1. How many acres of corn do the Yoders have? _____

2. Which crop is planted on 30 acres? _____

3. Which two crops are each planted on less than 30 acres? _____

4. Which crop takes up the most acres? _____

5. How many acres does Mr. Yoder use for wheat? _____

6. Did Mr. Yoder plant more acres of corn or soybeans? How many more?

_____

_____

Extension: Write a problem that uses data from the bar graph. Share it with a classmate.
Virginia Mathematics Standards of Learning: (3.22) Read and interpret data represented in bar and picture graphs.

Use with Chapter 1, Section A.   Virginia Connections **1**

Name _____

Ahoy! Whales to Starboard!

Whales can be seen in the Atlantic Ocean off the coast of Virginia. Twice a year the whales migrate along the coastline. In the fall, they swim to the warm waters in the South. In the spring, they swim back to the cooler waters in the North. Tourists can take boat trips to see the whales feed and play.

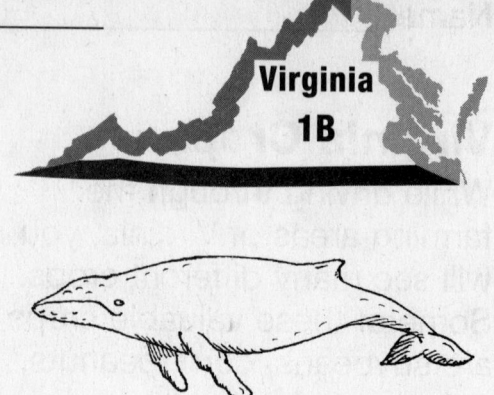

Virginia 1B

Jenny spent a week whale watching off the coast of Virginia. She made this tally table.

Whales Sighted on Weekdays	
Monday	卌 卌 卌 I
Tuesday	IIII
Wednesday	卌 卌 卌 卌
Thursday	卌 卌 II
Friday	卌 III

1. Use the data in the tally table to complete the pictograph.

Whales Sighted on Weekdays	
Monday	■ ■ ■ ■ ■ ■ ■ ■
Tuesday	
Wednesday	
Thursday	
Friday	

■ = 2 Whales

2. Suppose each symbol in the pictograph represents 4 whales.

   a. How many symbols would there be for whales sighted on Tuesday? _____

   b. on Thursday? _____

Extension: Ask your classmates to vote on their favorite marine animal. Use seals, sharks, whales, and dolphins. Collect the data in a tally table. Then make a bar graph of the data.
Virginia Mathematics Standards of Learning: (3.22) Read and interpret data represented in bar and picture graphs. (3.21) Given grid paper, collect data on a given topic and construct a bar graph showing the results. A title and key will will be included.

Name _____

Virginia's Cities

Virginia Beach is Virginia's largest city. It is the 35th largest city in the United States. Virginia has 3 cities that have a population of over 2,000,000 people.

Virginia 2A

Write the value of the underlined digit in the number that shows the population of each city.

City	Population	Value of Digit
1. Richmond	20<u>2</u>,798	_____
2. Virginia Beach	3<u>9</u>3,089	_____
3. Norfolk	<u>2</u>61,250	_____
4. Danville	53,05<u>6</u>	_____
5. Fairfax	19,<u>6</u>29	_____
6. Salem	23,7<u>9</u>7	_____
7. Lexington	<u>6</u>,959	_____
8. Covington	6,<u>9</u>91	_____

Write the number in standard form.

9. The population of Staunton is twenty-four thousand, four hundred sixty-one. _____

10. The population of Hampton is one hundred thirty-three thousand, eight hundred eleven. _____

11. There are 100,000 + 10,000 + 1,000 + 100 + 80 + 2 people living in Alexandria. _____

12. There are 100,000 + 3,000 + 900 + 10 people living in Portsmouth. _____

Extension: Find the population of a city near you. Write the number in standard and expanded form, and write the word name for it.
Virginia Mathematics Standards of Learning: (3.1) Read and write six digit numerals and identify the place value for each digit.

Use with Chapter 2, Section A.
Virginia Connections 3

Name _____

Virginia 2B

Vacation in Beautiful Virginia Beach

Virginia Beach is the largest resort beach in the world. It has 29 miles of beach that run along the coast of the Atlantic Ocean. Visitors can enjoy swimming, surfing, sunning, sailing, fishing, and diving. They can also visit the Virginia Marine Science Museum, the Oceana Naval Air Station, or Ocean Breeze Fun Park.

Miles from Virginia Beach	
Staunton	215 miles
Fairfax	207 miles
Petersburg	94 miles
Charlottesville	178 miles

This table shows how far some Virginia cities are from Virginia Beach.

1. Suzanne lives in Staunton. José lives in Fairfax. They both want to go to Virginia Beach.

   Who will have to travel farther to get to Virginia Beach? _____

2. Mrs. Owens' class is from Petersburg. Mr. Wymer's class is from Charlottesville. They are both planning field trips to the Virginia Marine Science Museum in Virginia Beach.

   Which class is closer? _____

3. How far does each class need to travel, rounded to the nearest 100 miles?

   a. Mrs. Owens' class in Petersburg _____

   b. Mr. Wymer's class in Charlottesville _____

4. List the names of the cities in the chart in order from the greatest to the least distance from Virginia Beach.

   _____

   _____

Extension: Find out how far you live from Virginia Beach. Write a sentence to compare your distance from Virginia Beach to the distance of one of the other Virginia cities from Virginia Beach.
Virginia Mathematics Standards of Learning: (3.3) Compare two whole numbers between 0 and 9,999. (3.8) Solve problems using the sum or difference of two whole numbers.

Virginia Connections

Use with Chapter 2, Section B.

Name _____

Virginia
2C

Sightseeing in Richmond

Richmond is the capital of Virginia. It is a city that provides many political, historical, cultural and educational sites. Many people visit Richmond because of these sites.

Sight	What to See
Monument Avenue	Statues of Robert E. Lee, Jefferson Davis, Stonewall Jackson, Arthur Ashe
Virginia Museum of Fine Arts	Paintings, sculptures, Fabergé eggs
Science Museum of Virginia	Planetarium shows and exhibits
Lewis Ginter Botanical Garden	Flowers, trees, shrubs
Maymont	Mansion, nature center, children's farm

Use the data in the table above to help you plan an afternoon of sightseeing in Richmond.

- Begin by going to the Monument Avenue statues. Then choose the other sights you want to see.
- You will go sightseeing from 12:00 P.M. to 5:00 P.M.
- Allow 15 minutes to get from one sight to the next.

Sight	Time to Arrive	Time to Leave
Monument Avenue	12:00 P.M.	1:00 P.M.
	1:15 P.M.	

Extension: It took the Johnson's 5 hours to drive to Richmond. If they left at 6:30 A.M., what time did they arrive in Richmond?

Virginia Mathematics Standards of Learning: (3.15) Tell time to the nearest five-minute interval and to the nearest minute.

Use with Chapter 2, Section C.

Virginia Connections

Name _____

Virginia's State Bird

Virginia 3A

The Virginia state bird is the cardinal. The cardinal is about 8 inches long and has a pointed feather crest on its head. The male cardinal is bright red with a black throat. The female is brown with red on its crest, wings, and tail. Both have red bills. Cardinals eat insects, weed seeds, and ripe berries.

Complete each exercise.

1. 8 insects + 3 insects = _____ insects

2. _____ insects + 30 insects = 110 insects

3. 800 insects + _____ insects = 1,100 insects

4. 7 seeds + 2 seeds = _____ seeds

5. _____ seeds + 20 seeds = 90 seeds

6. 700 seeds + _____ seeds = 900 seeds

7. 9 berries + 6 berries = _____ berries

8. _____ berries + 60 berries = 150 berries

9. 900 berries + _____ berries = 1,500 berries

10. 6 seeds + 5 seeds = _____ seeds

11. _____ seeds + 50 seeds = 110 seeds

12. 600 seeds + _____ seeds = 1,100 seeds

13. What patterns do you see in these exercises?

_____

_____

Extension: 20 cardinals + ____ cardinals = 50 cardinals
Virginia Mathematics Standards of Learning: (3.8) Solve problems involving the sum of two whole numbers. (3.24) Recognize and describe patterns formed.

6 Virginia Connections   Use with Chapter 3, Section A.

Name _____

How Far is It?

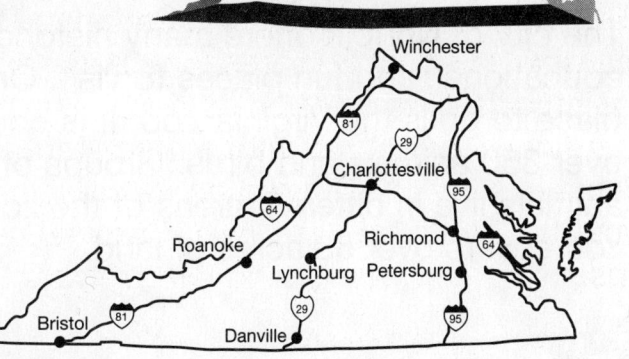

Traveling by bus, car, barge, train, airplane, or boat is possible in Virginia. Richmond and Charlottesville are where many of the state roads meet. Major highways in Virginia are I-81, I-64, I-95, and U.S. 29.

Distances Between Virginia Cities	
Bristol to Roanoke	148 miles
Charlottesville to Richmond	71 miles
Danville to Lynchburg	67 miles
Roanoke to Winchester	178 miles
Richmond to Petersburg	23 miles

Solve each problem.

1. A bus with passengers travels from Danville to Lynchburg. It then returns to Danville. How far does it travel? _____ miles

2. Trace the route on the map with a blue marker.

3. A truck loaded with food travels from Bristol to Roanoke and then to Winchester. How far does it travel? _____ miles

4. Trace the route on the map with a red marker.

5. Write your own problem. Use the data in the table. Write a question that can be answered by using addition.

_____

_____

Extension: Sally drove from Charlottesville to Richmond and then to Petersburg. How many miles did she travel? Trace the route on the map with a green marker.
Virginia Mathematics Standards of Learning: (3.8) Solve problems involving the sum or difference of two whole numbers, with or without regrouping.

Use with Chapter 3, Section B. Virginia Connections

Name _____

Virginia
3C

Let's Go to the Zoo

The city of Norfolk offers many historical, educational, and fun places to visit. One place to go is the Virginia Zoo. It is home to over 350 animals and birds. Groups of animals live in different areas of the zoo. The zoo covers over 53 acres of land.

Use the data in the tables to answer each question.

Admission	
Adults	$3.50
Children	$1.75

Food	
Hot Dog	$2.75
Hamburger	$4.25
Grilled Cheese Sandwich	$3.25
French Fries	$1.75
Soft Drinks	$1.25

Gifts	
Tiger Shoe Laces	$3.75
Zebra Key Chain	$4.25
Lion Book	$6.98
Gazelle Knapsack	$7.99
Monkey Pencil	$1.39

1. How much would a hot dog and a soft drink cost together? _____

2. How much would admission for 2 children cost? _____

3. Michelle has $10. Name 2 gifts she can buy. _____

_____

4. Dan wants to buy tiger shoe laces and a gazelle knapsack. He has $13. Does Dan have enough money to buy both items? Explain.

_____

5. Tamitha has $12. Can she buy 2 lion books? Explain.

_____

6. Janet spent exactly $5 on lunch. What two items did she buy?

_____

Extension: Use the data in the tables to write a problem. Ask a classmate to solve your problem.
Virginia Mathematics Standards of Learning: (4.5) Solve problems involving addition of money.

Name _____

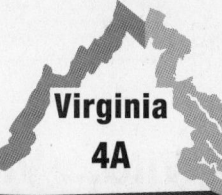

Virginia
4A

What's in the Woods?

Forests and mountains cover much of Virginia. Oak, pine, walnut, locust, gum, and poplar trees grow in the forests. Many animals make the forests their home.

Solve the puzzle to find the names of some of the animals that live in Virginia. Subtract. Then write the letter on the line above the matching answer. Not all the letters are used.

1. 87 − 79   _____ B
2. 97 − 69   _____ R
3. 38 − 8   _____ K
4. 75 − 10   _____ A
5. $65 − $27 _____ N
6. 60 − 40   _____ C
7. $50 − $30 _____ E
8. 45 − 12   _____ O
9. 98 − 25   _____ U
10. $49 − $21 _____ L
11. 89 − 54   _____ T
12. $77 − $41 _____ D

___ ___ ___ ___ ___   ___ ___ ___ ___
 8 $28 65 20 30   8 $20 65 28

___ ___ ___ ___ ___ ___ ___
28 65 20 20 33 33 $38

___ ___ ___ ___ ___ ___
 8 33   8 20 65 35

___ ___ ___ ___
$36 $20 $20 28

Extension: Make a subtraction puzzle about other animals that live in Virginia. Share it with the class.
Virginia Mathematics Standards of Learning: (3.8) Solve problems involving the sum or difference of two whole numbers, with or without regrouping.

Use with Chapter 4, Section A.   Virginia Connections   **9**

Name _____

Go Wild... Visit Virginia's Natural Area Preserve Sites

Virginia 4B

The Virginia Natural Area Preserve System was established in the late 1980's to protect the land and animals of Virginia. These preserves include some of the rarest natural communities and rare species habitats in Virginia. The Preserve System is made up of 21 natural areas that total 11,833 acres.

Solve each problem.

1. Hughlett Point and New Point Comfort Preserve both contain parts of Tiger Beetle Beach. Hughlett Point has 204 acres. New Point Comfort has 109 acres. How many more acres does Hughlett Point have? _____

2. Northwest River and North Landing River Preserve both have swamps. Northwest River has 2,244 acres. North Landing River has 2,577 acres. How many more acres does North Landing River have? _____

3. Cowbane Prairie is 63 acres. Big Spring Bog is 50 acres. How many more acres does Cowbane Prairie have? _____

4. Pinnacle is 198 acres. Chub Sandhill is 387 acres. How many more acres does Chub Sandhill have? _____

5. Cowbane Prairie has how many fewer acres than Chub Sandhill? _____

Extension: Cape Charles Coastal Habitat consists of 29 acres of coastal beach, dunes and maritime forests. Johnson Creek, a 99 acre preserve, is home to rare plants, such as Shale Barren Rockcress. How many more acres does Johnson Creek have?

Virginia Mathematics Standards of Learning: (3.8) Solve problems involving the sum or difference of two whole numbers, with or without regrouping.

Name _____

Sights Along Route 5

Virginia 4C

Route 5 is one of the most scenic highways in America. There are 9 historic plantations, historic houses, and beautiful gardens along this route. Benjamin Harrison was born at one of the plantations. He signed the Declaration of Independence. William Henry Harrison, the 9th president, was born there, also.

Solve the puzzle to find the name of this plantation. Subtract. Then write the letter on the line above the matching answer at the bottom of the page.

1. 126   I
   − 49

2. 4,562   E
   − 486

3. 6,420   N
   − 3,927

4. $1.79   A
   − 0.86

5. $5.68   T
   − 2.34

6. $9.86   P
   − 4.97

7. $10.47 O
   − 8.59

8. $16.46 L
   − 13.59

9. $2,558 Y
   − 389

10. 8,602   B
   − 6,003

11. $9.50   R
   − 4.36

12. $9.99   K
   − 4.58

The ___ ___ ___ ___ ___ ___ ___ ___
   2,599 4,076 $5.14 $5.41 4,076 $2.87 4,076 $2,169

___ ___ ___ ___ ___ ___ ___ ___ ___
$4.89 $2.87 $0.93 2,493 $3.34 $0.93 $3.34 77 $1.88 2,493

Extension: Make a subtraction puzzle about another Virginia plantation. Share it with the class.
Virginia Mathematics Standards of Learning: (3.8) Solve problems involving the sum or difference of whole numbers, with or without regrouping.

Use with Chapter 4, Section C.   Virginia Connections **11**

Name _____

Fishing in Virginia

Virginia 5A

There are many places to go fishing in Virginia. Smith Mountain Lake, Claytor Lake, Lake Anna, Buggs Island, and Lake Moomaw are all great places to catch fish.

Write an addition sentence and a multiplication sentence for each story

1. The Johnson family went fishing. There are 5 people in the family. Each caught 4 fish. How many fish did the family catch?

   ___ + ___ + ___ + ___ + ___ = ___

   ___ × ___ = ___

2. The members of the Alvarez family each caught 5 fish. There are 3 people in the family. How many fish did the Alvarez family catch?

   ___ + ___ + ___ = ___

   ___ × ___ = ___

3. Draw a picture that shows 2 × 6 fish. Find the product.

   ___ × ___ = ___

Extension: If each person in your family caught 3 fish, how many fish would that be?
Virginia Mathematics Standards of Learning: (3.9) Recall multiplication and division facts through the nines table. (3.10) Create and solve problems that involve multiplication of two whole numbers.

Name _____

Mmmm! Yum, Yum!

Apples are one of the fruits grown in Virginia. Many desserts have apples in them. You can find many of these desserts at the Apple Harvest Arts and Crafts Festival in Winchester.

Cameron and Michael are going to invite 20 of their friends over for an apple pie party. They have to find out how many pies to make so that their friends each get a slice of their delicious apple pie.

On a separate sheet of paper, draw a picture to help you solve the problems.

1. Cameron and Michael's recipe for apple pie makes 2 pies.

   a. If each pie is cut into 6 slices, how many pieces of pie will Cameron and Michael have? _____

   b. If each pie is cut into 8 slices, how many pieces of pie will Cameron and Michael have? _____

2. Suppose all 20 people invited to the party, along with Carmeron and Michael, want a piece of pie.

   a. If each pie is cut into 6 pieces, will 3 pies be enough? _____

   b. If each pie is cut into 8 pieces, will 3 pies be enough? _____

Extension: Find out how many pies are needed for thirty-two (32) people, if each pie is cut into eight (8) slices.
Virginia Mathematics Standards of Learning: (3.9) Recall multiplication and division facts through the nines table.

Use with Chapter 5, Section B.　　　　　　　　　　　Virginia Connections　**13**

Name _____

A Garden Wonderland

The Norfolk Botanical Garden has a large collection of colorful rhododendrons, azaleas, tulips, roses and many other beautiful flowers. The garden has over 20 theme gardens on 155 acres. This is the only botanical garden in the nation that can be toured by boat and by train.

Boat ride through the Norfolk Botanical Garden

Virginia 6A

Solve the puzzle to find out more about the Norfolk Botanical Garden. Find each product. Write the letter on the line above the matching answer.

1. 8 × 9 = __72__ T   **2.** 9 × 7 = __63__ O   **3.** 7 × 2 = __14__ H

4. 4 × 8 = __32__ E   **5.** 6 × 4 = __24__ M   **6.** 4 × 7 = __28__ I

7. 9 × 4 = __36__ R   **8.** 3 × 7 = __21__ S   **9.** 8 × 5 = __40__ N

10. 6 × 7 = __42__ A   **11.** 7 × 5 = __35__ L   **12.** 2 × 6 = __12__ W

13. 3 × 5 = __15__ Y   **14.** 8 × 7 = __56__ B   **15.** 7 × 7 = __49__ G

"__T__ __H__ __E__ __R__ __E__   __I__ __S__
 72   14   32   36   32   28   21

__S__ __O__ __M__ __E__ __T__ __H__ __I__ __N__ __G__
 21   63   24   32   72   14   28   40   49

__A__ __L__ __W__ __A__ __Y__ __S__
 42   35   12   42   15   21

__I__ __N__   __B__ __L__ __O__ __O__ __M__."
 28   40   56   35   63   63   24

Extension: Find other flowers that grow in Virginia and make a multiplication puzzle. Share it with the class.
Virginia Mathematics Standards of Learning: (3.9) Recall the multiplication and division facts through the nines table.

Name _____

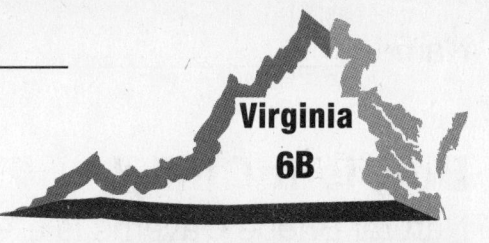

Cultivate America's Roots

At the Museum of American Frontier Culture in Staunton, Virginia, visitors can learn about the lives of early Virginians through four different farms. Three show the types of farms America's early settlers left behind in Germany, Ireland, and England. The fourth farm shows how the settlers combined all their farming ideas into one American farm.

Make a table or draw a picture to solve each problem.

1. Three German families with 5 members each came to America to settle. How many people came in all?

   _____

2. A covered wagon can carry 6 people. How many wagons would be needed for 45 people?

   _____

3. Suppose a farmer wants to grow 40 stalks of corn. If he can plant 8 stalks in each row, how many rows does he need to plant?

   _____

Extension: Draw a picture of a corn field. Make up a multiplication problem to describe the field.
Virginia Mathematics Standards of Learning: (3.9) Recall the multiplication and division facts through the nines table.

Use with Chapter 6, Section B.   Virginia Connections **15**

Name _____

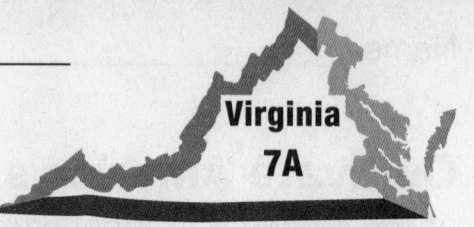

Boy, is it Chilly!

Natural Bridge Caverns is a Virginia cave that goes 347 feet into the earth. The cave stays at 54 degrees all year. While touring the caves, you will see Mirror Lake, the Waterfall Room, the Canyon Room, the Wishing Well Room, and the Colossal Dome Room.

Solve. You may use counters or draw pictures to help.

1. Tom has 15 pictures he took in the Wishing Well Room. He wants to share the pictures equally among 5 people in his family. How many pictures will each person get? _____

2. Sally has 21 pictures she took in the Waterfall Room. If she keeps 5 of the pictures and shares the others equally among 4 friends, how many will each friend receive? _____

3. Seven third-grade girls took 42 pictures total. If they share the pictures equally, how many pictures will each girl receive? _____

4. Ms. Harrison took 20 pictures of Mirror Lake.

   a. Can she share them equally among 5 people? Explain.

   _____

   b. Can she share them equally among 3 people? Explain.

   _____

Extension: Write 2 problems about Natural Bridge Caverns. Ask a classmate to solve your problems.
Virginia Mathematics Standards of Learning: (3.9) Recall the multiplication and division facts through the nines table.

Name _____

The First Free School

Hampton had the first free school in America. Benjamin Syms and Thomas Eaton both gave land to the people of Hampton for the school. Later, the school was named the Syms-Eaton Academy. This was the beginning of free public education in America.

Virginia 7B

Solve each problem.

1. There are 24 chairs in the art room. There are 4 chairs at each table. How many tables are there?

   _____

2. The class is making a total of 40 puppets. Each student is making 5 puppets. How many students are in the class?

   _____

3. There is a total of 28 paintings on the bulletin boards all together. Each board has 4 paintings. How many bulletin boards are there?

   _____

4. Each package of felt has 5 pieces. Mr. Jackson needs 45 pieces of red felt. How many packages does he need to order?

   _____

5. There are 18 paint brushes. Each child will clean 3. How many children will be needed to clean all the brushes?

   _____

6. Wheat paste for paper maché comes in 4 pound bags. Mrs. Barton ordered 32 pounds. How many bags did she order?

   _____

Extension: If mechanical pencils cost $2 each and you have $10, how many mechanical pencils can you buy?
Virginia Mathematics Standards of Learning: (3.9) Recall the multiplication and division facts through the nines table.

Use with Chapter 7, Section B.

Virginia Connections **17**

Name _____

Home of the Original Ice-Cream Cone

Virginia 7C

The first ice-cream cone was created by Abe Doumar at the 1904 St. Louis Exposition. It was made of a rolled-up wafer and was called the "ice-cream cornucopia." The cones became so popular that in 1907, Mr. Doumar opened a shop in Ocean View, Virginia. This shop sold 22,600 cones in a single day! Today, Doumar's Drive-in is run by Abe's nephew, Al Doumar, and is located in Norfolk.

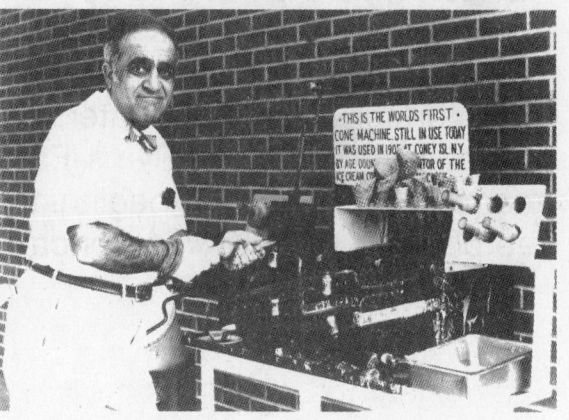

The first ice-cream cone machine

1. Shade the odd numbers in the chart to learn how many flavors of ice cream are served at the Doumar's Drive-In in Norfolk.

12	47	33	63	20
18	20	56	21	8
10	80	30	45	64
32	54	42	97	16
24	18	74	63	48

2. Since 8 × 7 = 56, 56 ÷ 8 = _____, and 56 ÷ 7 = _____ .

3. Since 7 × 6 = 42, 42 ÷ 7 = _____, and 42 ÷ 6 = _____ .

4. Since 8 × 4 = 32, 32 ÷ 8 = _____, and 32 ÷ 4 = _____ .

5. Since 6 × 9 = 54, 54 ÷ 6 = _____, and 54 ÷ 9 = _____ .

6. Since 9 × 8 = 72, 72 ÷ 9 = _____, and 72 ÷ 8 = _____ .

Extension: Find the favorite flavors of ice cream of the students in your class. Make a bar graph to show their favorite flavors.
Virginia Mathematics Standards of Learning: (3.9) Recall the multiplication and division facts through the nines table. (3.4) Recognize and use the inverse relationships between multiplication/division to complete basic fact sentences.

Name _____

What a Kick!

If you are a soccer fan, Richmond is the city for you. In 1993, Richmond received its own Division II Professional Soccer team—the Richmond Kickers. Not only do the Richmond Kickers provide high quality soccer, but they also provide soccer camps for the boys and girls in the community.

Virginia
8A

Draw lines of symmetry on each soccer item.

1. Soccer Ball   **2.** Soccer Shorts   **3.** Soccer Shirt

4. Water Bottle   **5.** Soccer Field   **6.** Soccer Goal

Does each of the following letters in the word Kickers appear to have a line of symmetry? Write yes or no.

7. K _____   **8.** I _____   **9.** C _____   **10.** K _____

11. E _____   **12.** R _____   **13.** S _____

Extension: Print your name. Which letters have one or more lines of symmetry?
Virginia Mathematics Standards of Learning: (3.20) Given appropriate drawings or models, identify and describe congruent and symmetrical two-dimensional figures.

Use with Chapter 8, Section A.   Virginia Connections   **19**

Name _____

Explore Virginia

In size, Virginia ranks 35th among the states in the United States. That means there are 34 states larger than Virginia and 15 states smaller. Virginia's total area of 42,777 square miles includes 24,778 square miles of forests. The natural beauty of the mountains, valleys, and coastal plain has made Virginia a favorite place for tourists to explore.

The Blue Ridge Mountains

Use the map below to estimate the area of Virginia in square units.

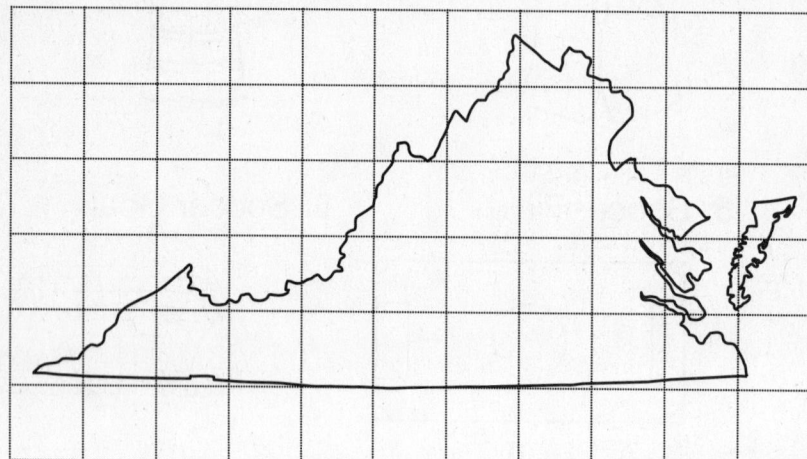

1. Count the number of squares that are completely inside Virginia. _____

2. Estimate the rest of the area by counting partly covered squares together. About how many whole squares can you make out of partly covered squares? _____

3. Estimate the total area of Virginia in square units. _____

Extension: On grid paper draw a rectangle with a perimeter of 12 units. Find its area. Draw another rectangle with a perimeter of 12 units and a different area.
Virginia Mathematics Standards of Learning: (2.13) Estimate and then count the number of square units needed to cover a given surface (determine area).

20 Virginia Connections

Use with Chapter 8, Section B.

Name _____

Virginia
9A

Busch Gardens Williamsburg

Busch Gardens in Williamsburg was voted "America's Most Beautiful Theme Park" for 6 straight years. The park has a 17th century European theme. It has the world's tallest, fastest, most twisted inverted roller coaster called the "Alpengeist."

Estimate to solve each problem.

1. Buses of students arrive for a day of fun. Each bus holds 41 students.

   About how many students can 7 buses hold? _____

2. Dave sells ice cream bars in one section of the park. He sold 287 bars on Monday.

   About how many bars will he sell in 5 days? _____

3. Just before the "Pirates" show begins, Patty sees 4 people selling large paper flowers. Each person is holding 16 paper flowers.

   About how many paper flowers are there in all? _____

4. There are 3 trains for the "Alpengeist" roller coaster. Each train holds 32 people.

   About how many people can all 3 trains hold? _____

5. 28 people ride a roller coaster 4 times each.

   About how many rides were taken on the roller coaster? _____

Extension: Write your own multiplication problem about Busch Gardens in Williamsburg. Ask a classmate to solve your problem.
Virginia Mathematics Standards of Learning: (3.10) Solve problems that involve multiplication of two whole numbers, one factor 99 or less and the second factor 5 or less.

Use with Chapter 9, Section A.

Name _____

How Many Passes?

On February 3rd, 1940, in the city of Richmond, a future football star was born. He threw 342 touchdown passes in his career. That is more than any other quarterback has thrown. He played for the Minnesota Vikings and the New York Giants. In 1986 he was elected into the Pro Football Hall of Fame.

Virginia 9B

Solve the puzzle to find the name of this famous player. Multiply. Then write the letter on the line above the matching answer. Not all letters are used.

1. 96 × 4 = ____ S   2. 32 × 4 = ____ R   3. 85 × 8 = ____ C

4. 76 × 9 = ____ A   5. 99 × 9 = ____ B   6. 54 × 7 = ____ I

7. 83 × 6 = ____ E   8. 36 × 8 = ____ K   9. 67 × 8 = ____ G

10. 56 × 5 = ____ T   11. 95 × 3 = ____ O   12. 64 × 7 = ____ F

13. 82 × 4 = ____ N   14. 57 × 4 = ____ U   15. 83 × 7 = ____ M

___ ___ ___ ___
448 128 684 328

___ ___ ___ ___ ___ ___ ___ ___ ___
280 684 128 288 498 328 280 285 328

Extension: Use a calculator to find the greatest number you can multiply by 35 to get a product less than 800.
Virginia Mathematics Standards of Learning: (3.10) Solve problems that involve multiplication of two whole numbers, one factor 99 or less and the second factor 5 or less.

Name _____

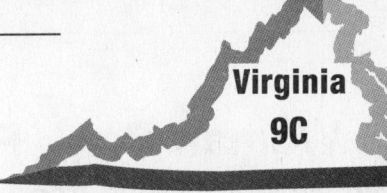

NASCAR County

Richmond International Raceway held its first race on October 12, 1946. At that time, the track was $\frac{1}{2}$ mile long and made of dirt. Now the track is $\frac{3}{4}$ mile long and paved. Each year the Raceway holds two NASCAR Winston Cup Series races.

Solve each problem.

1. David has 34 model cars to display on shelves in his room. Each shelf holds 6 cars. He fills one shelf before he begins another.

    a. How many shelves have 6 model cars? _____

    b. How many model cars are left for the next shelf? _____

2. Amy has 27 model cars to put in display boxes in her room. Each box holds 8 cars. She fills one box before she begins another.

    a. How many display boxes have 8 model cars? _____

    b. How many model cars are left for the next display box? _____

3. Brian has 53 race-car postcards. His postcard album will hold 8 postcards on a page.

    a. How many full pages are used? _____

    b. How many postcards are left for the next page? _____

    c. How many more postcards would Brian need to fill 10 pages? _____

4. David wants to buy a set of model cars that costs $48. He decides to save the same amount of money each week for 8 weeks to buy the set. How much must he save each week? _____

Extension: Write your own division problem about a collection in which the remainder is 3. Share your problem with a classmate.
Virginia Mathematics Standards of Learning: (3.9) Recall division facts through the nines table.

Name _____

First Woman Bank President

Maggie Walker was an important African American in Virginia history. She opened a bank in 1903 and became the first female bank president in America. Today the bank is called the Consolidated Bank and Trust and is located in Richmond.

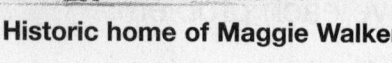
Virginia 10A

Historic home of Maggie Walker

Estimate the amount of each dollar bill that is shaded.

1.  _____

2.  _____

3.  _____

Color each rectangle.

4. $\frac{1}{4}$ green

5. $\frac{3}{8}$ green

6. What fraction of the rectangle is

white? _____ gray? _____ black? _____

Extension: Draw a rectangle. Color $\frac{3}{5}$ red, $\frac{1}{5}$ green, and $\frac{1}{5}$ orange.
Virginia Mathematics Standards of Learning: (3.5) Name and write the fractions represented by drawings or concrete materials and represent a given fraction, using concrete material and symbols.

24 Virginia Connections   Use with Chapter 10, Section A.

Name _____

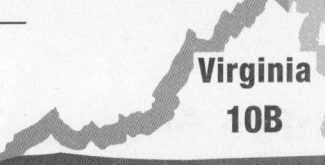

A Young Man's Invention

Cyrus McCormick was born near Staunton, Virginia in 1809. In July 1831, Cyrus introduced a new farm machine that would make harvesting crops go much faster. He called the machine a reaper. The reaper could harvest a field of wheat in 3 hours that would have taken 5 days to do by hand! The reaper helped farmers everywhere.

Cyrus McCormick and his reaper

Solve. Use counters or draw pictures to help.

1. Mr. Williams harvested $\frac{1}{3}$ of the 27 fields he had planted. How many fields did he harvest? _____

2. Mr. Smith planted $\frac{1}{4}$ of his 24 fields with corn. How many corn fields did he plant? _____

3. Mr. Williams spent $\frac{1}{5}$ of his money on farm supplies. If he started with $20, how much money did he spend? _____

4. Mr. Smith used $\frac{1}{6}$ of his 12 horses to pull a wagon. How many horses did he use? _____

5. In a month Mr. Williams harvested 15 fields of wheat. If he harvested $\frac{1}{3}$ of them in one week, how many did he harvest that week? _____

Extension: Bread is baked in loaves and is delicious when served hot. Draw a set of loaves of bread to represent each mixed number: $1\frac{1}{2}$, $2\frac{1}{4}$, $1\frac{3}{4}$.
Virginia Mathematics Standards of Learning: (6.6) Solve problems that involve multiplication with fractions.

Name _____

Virginia's Festive Festivals

Each year, many exciting festivals are held throughout Virginia. Some of these festivals celebrate the strawberry season. At the Pungo Strawberry festival in Virginia Beach, you can see a parade and enjoy live music. At the Oak Grove Strawberry Festival, you can pick your own strawberries and enter a pie-eating contest. Virginians love strawberries!.

A farmer planted a small field of strawberries. Look at this garden plan to answer the questions. Note that the plan shows measurements in yards, while many of the questions ask for measurements in feet or inches.

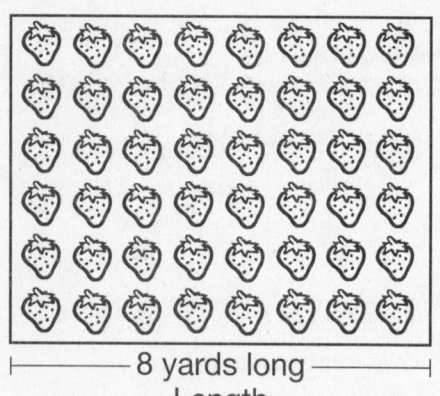

🍓 = one strawberry plant

6 yards deep
Width

8 yards long
Length

1. What is the length of the garden in feet? _____

2. What is the width of the garden in feet? _____

3. How much longer is the length than the width in yards? _____

    In feet? _____ In inches? _____

4. What is the garden's perimeter in yards? _____ In feet? _____

5. If the farmer planted 1 more column of strawberry plants along the left side, what would the perimeter be in feet? _____
(Hint: Draw a picture.)

Extension: Design a garden of your choice that has a perimeter of 18 feet.
Virginia Mathematics Standards of Learning: (3.10) Solve problems that involve multiplication of two whole numbers. (3.14) Use measuring devices with metric and U.S. customary units.

Name _____

Virginia
11A

What's Glowing on the Mountain?

Roanoke, located in Shenandoah Valley, is known as the "Star City of the South." Because of this nickname, the citizens of Roanoke built a giant, eighty-eight and a half foot tall star on top of Mill Mountain. This star is the world's largest man-made illuminated star!

Solve the problems to find the meaning of "Shenandoah." Maybe this is what helped give Roanoke its nickname.

Write the letter next to each exercise above its equivalent decimal below.

1. $2\frac{3}{10} =$ ____ U
2. $7\frac{11}{100} =$ ____ O
3. $3\frac{75}{100} =$ ____ E

4. $5\frac{1}{10} =$ ____ H
5. $2\frac{21}{100} =$ ____ D
6. $1\frac{9}{100} =$ ____ S

7. $2\frac{7}{10} =$ ____ T
8. $2\frac{3}{100} =$ ____ R
9. $4\frac{83}{100} =$ ____ G

10. $5\frac{63}{100} =$ ____ F
11. $1\frac{9}{10} =$ ____ A
12. $2\frac{30}{100} =$ ____ U

___ ___ ___ ___ ___ ___ ___ ___
2.21 1.9 2.3 4.83 5.1 2.7 3.75 2.03

___ ___   ___ ___ ___
7.11 5.63   2.7 5.1 3.75

___ ___ ___ ___ ___
1.09 2.7 1.9 2.03 1.09

Extension: Make your own decimal puzzle about a special place in Virginia. Share it with the class.
Virginia Mathematics Standards of Learning: (3.7) Read and write decimals expressed as tenths and hundredths, using concrete materials.

Use with Chapter 11, Section A.

Virginia Connections 27

Name _____

The Historic Triangle

Just north of Hampton is an area called the Historic Triangle. Jamestown, Yorktown, and Williamsburg are the 3 cities that make up the triangle. Many famous events from early America took place in this little triangle. In Jamestown, visitors can see a full-size model of the ship that brought over the first colonists, and in Williamsburg, they can see the town's restored buildings.

Virginia
11B

Write whether you would measure each in cm, m, or km.

1. The height of the statue of Pocahontas _____

2. The width of a tri-corned hat _____

3. The height of a giant oak tree _____

4. The distance from Jamestown to Williamsburg _____

5. The width of the ship, Discovery _____

6. The height of the Yorktown Victory Monument _____

7. The length of the York River _____

8. The length across the button of an officer's uniform _____

9. The width of a horse's hoof _____

10. The length of a drummer's drumstick _____

Extension: Name 2 other things you could measure using each unit: cm, m, km.
Virginia Mathematics Standards of Learning: (3.14) Estimate and then use actual measuring devices with metric and U.S. customary units to measure length.

28 Virginia Connections

Use with Chapter 11, Section B.

Name _____

What is a Goober?

A goober? A groundnut? An earthnut? These are all names for a peanut. Peanuts grow well in the soil along the Coastal Plains of Virginia. Emporia, Virginia holds a Peanut Festival to celebrate this important crop. Many uses of the peanut can be found in your own home: peanuts, peanut butter, ink, soap, shaving cream, paints, and animal feed.

Choose the better estimate for each.

1.
   a. 12 lb
   b. 12 oz

2.
   a. 1 pint
   b. 1 gallon

3.
   a. 100 kg
   b. 100 g

4.
   a. 1 cup
   b. 1 quart

5.
   a. 5 lb
   b. 5 oz

6.
   a. 1 L
   b. 1 mL

Extension: Make a list of peanut products in your home. Tell how they are measured.
Virginia Mathematics Standards of Learning: (3.14) Estimate and then use actual measuring devices with metric and U.S. customary units to measure: length-inches, feet, yards, centimeters, and meters; liquid volume-cups, pints, quarts, gallons, and liters; and weight/mass-ounces, pounds, grams, and kilograms.

Use with Chapter 12, Section A.

Name _____

Music Festivals

Virginia
12B

Music festivals are popular in Virginia towns. Galax, Virginia is home to the Old Fiddler's Convention. It is held for 3 days during the second week of August. Instruments such as guitars, mandolins, old-time fiddles, and bluegrass banjos can be seen at the festival.

Cheryl and Maggie went to the Old Fiddler's Convention last August. They each made a spinner to play an instrument game.

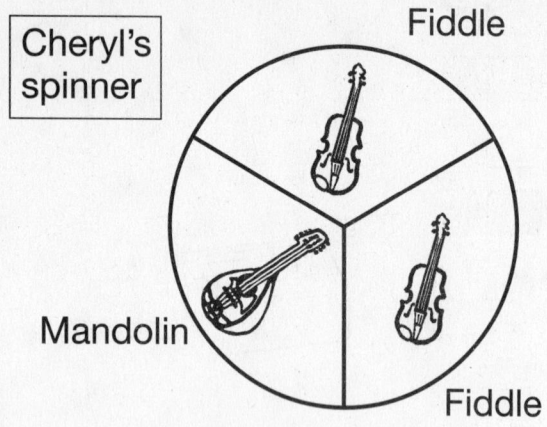

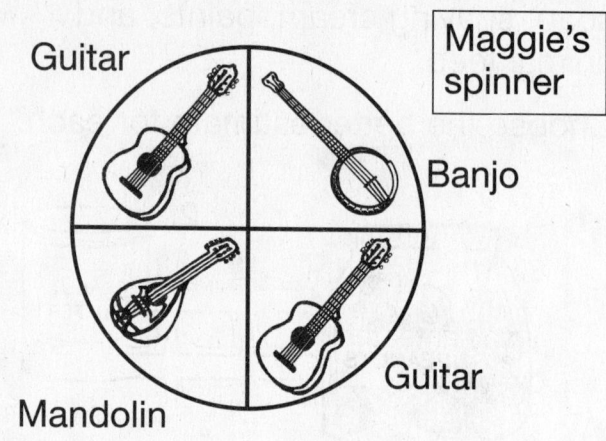

1. List the possible outcomes for each spinner.

    a. Cheryl's spinner _____

    b. Maggie's spinner _____

2. Predict which instrument each spinner is more likely to land on.

    a. Cheryl's spinner _____

    b. Maggie's spinner _____

3. Label the spinner to the right so that the probability of spinning a guitar is $\frac{1}{4}$, the probability of spinning a fiddle is $\frac{1}{4}$, and the probability of spinning a mandolin is $\frac{2}{4}$.

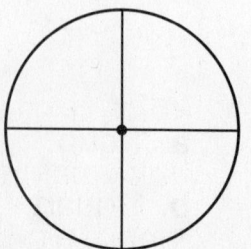

Extension: Draw a spinner using 4 instruments so that there is an equal likelihood of landing on each. Explain how you know that the spinner is fair.
Virginia Mathematics Standards of Learning: (3.23) Investigate and describe the concept of probability as chance and list possible results of a given situation.

Reading Pictographs

Use the pictograph to answer each question.

Sleepy Animals

Animal	Average Hours of Sleep a Day
Armadillo	8½ symbols
Cat	5½ symbols
Hamster	7 symbols
Koala	11 symbols
Lemur	8 symbols
Opossum	9½ symbols
Pig	4½ symbols
Sloth	10 symbols
Spiny anteater	6 symbols
Squirrel	7 symbols

⌒ = 2 hours of sleep

1. Which animal sleeps the most? _____
2. Which two animals get the same amount of sleep each day. _____
3. Which animal sleeps 16 hours per day? _____
4. How many more hours per day does a koala sleep than a pig? _____
5. How many animals sleep more than 12 hours? _____
6. Which animal sleeps exactly 12 hours? _____
7. Which animal sleeps the least? _____
8. Suppose a dog sleeps 6 hours per day. How many symbols would the dog have? _____

Name _____

Practice 1-2

Reading Bar Graphs

Use the bar graph to answer each question.

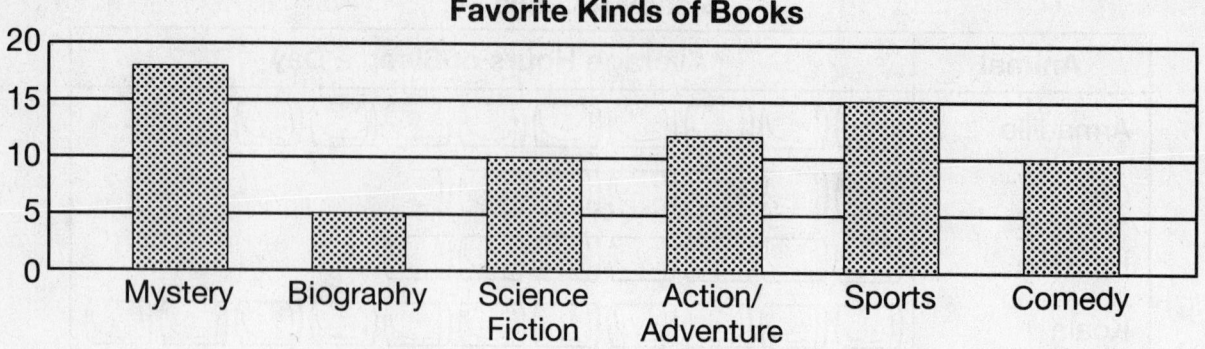

Favorite Kinds of Books

1. How many people chose sports books as their favorite? _____
2. Which kind of book is the favorite of all? _____
3. Which kind of book is the least favorite? _____
4. Do more people like sports books or science fiction books? Explain.
   _____
   _____
5. Which kind of book has 12 votes? _____
6. Which two kinds of books have the same number of votes?
   _____
7. Which kinds of book have over 13 votes?
   _____
8. Which kinds of books have less then 12 votes?
   _____
9. If 5 more people chose comedies as their favorite books, which kind of book would be the favorite of all?
   _____
10. If you voted, which kind of book would you vote for?
    _____

Name _____

Practice 1-3

Reading Line Graphs

Use the line graph to answer each question.

A hot tub holds many gallons of water. Cold water is put into the tub and warmed slowly. This graph shows how long it will take for water to reach 100 degrees. You don't want the water in a hot tub much warmer than 100 degrees or it would be too hot.

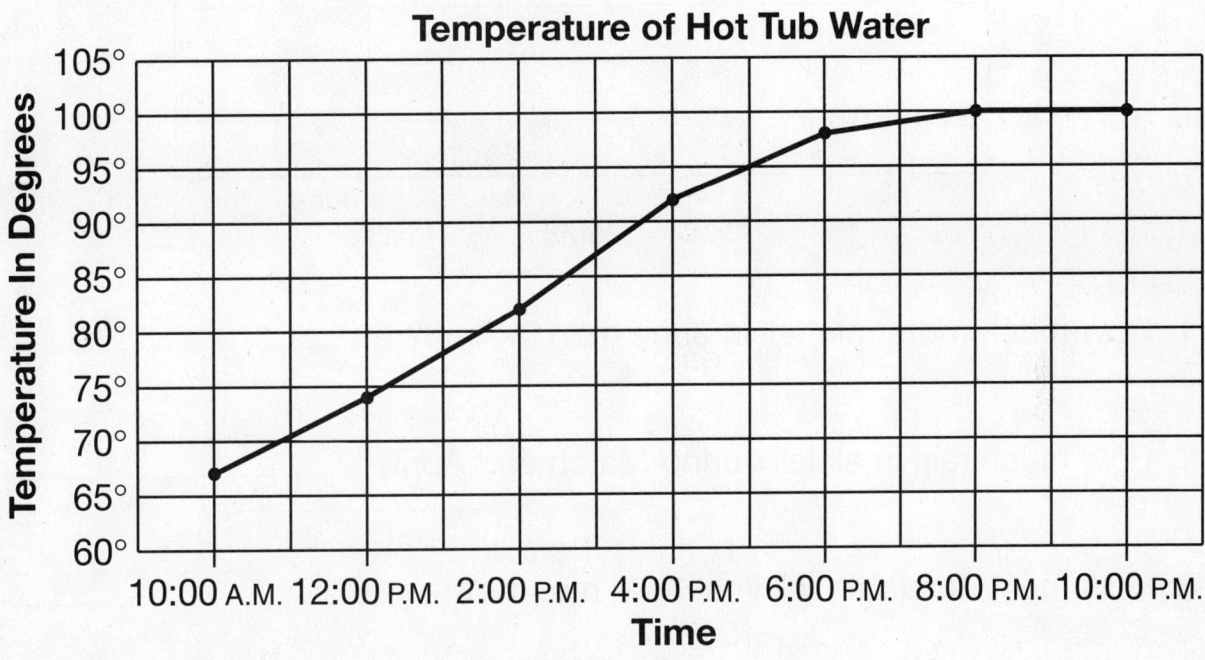

1. How hot was the water at 10:00 A.M.? _____

2. At what time was the water about 74°? _____

3. How many degrees did the water change between 10:00 A.M. and 12:00 P.M.? _____

4. How many degrees did the water change between 12:00 P.M. and 2:00 P.M.? _____

5. At what time was the water about 92°? _____

6. When did the water reach 100°? _____

7. What happened to the temperature of the water between 8:00 P.M. and 10:00 P.M.? _____

Analyze Word Problems: Introduction to Problem Solving

Plan how you will solve each problem. Then solve.

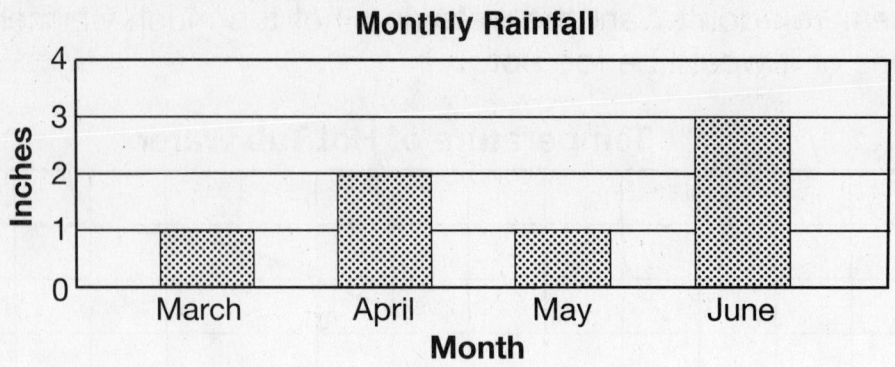

1. How much more rain fell in June than in April? _____

2. How much rain in all fell during March and April? _____

3. How much total rain fell in all four months? _____

4. If there was 2 inches more rain in July than there was in April, how much rain was there in July? _____

5. Which 2 months combined had the same amount of rainfall as there was in April? _____

6. Which month had twice as much rain as March? _____

7. Which month had three times as much rain as March? _____

Practice 1-5

Analyze Word Problems: Choose an Operation

Choose the number sentence you would use to solve. Explain.

1. Sam owns 3 lizards and 2 cats. How many pets does Sam own?

   a. $3 + 2 = 5$ **b.** $3 - 2 = 1$

2. Lisa moved 9 boxes. On Monday, she unpacked 5 boxes. How many more boxes are left to unpack?

   a. $9 + 5 = 14$ **b.** $9 - 5 = 4$

3. Tony baked 4 dozen muffins in the morning and 3 dozen more in the afternoon. How many dozen muffins did he bake in one day?

   a. $4 + 3 = 7$ **b.** $4 - 3 = 1$

Write which operation you would use. Then solve.

4. Sarah bought 10 cherries on Saturday. On Sunday, she ate 5. How many cherries does she have now?

5. Francis bought 7 cans of beans and 6 cans of corn. How many cans did he buy?

6. Judy is in a 10-kilometer road race. She has run 6 kilometers already. How many more kilometers will she run?

Name _____

Practice 1-6

Exploring Algebra: What's the Rule?

1. A rule describes what to do to the **In** number to get the **Out** number. What is the rule? _____

In	8	9	10	11	12	13
Out	5	6	7	8	9	10

Complete each table. Write the rule for each.

2.

In	4	6	2	5	10	8
Out	8	10	6			

Rule: _____

3.

In	8	4	3	5	11	6
Out	6	2	1			

Rule: _____

4.

In	10	7	6	4	12	3
Out	15	12	11			

Rule: _____

5.

In	9	11	8	4	6	7
Out	5	7	4			

Rule: _____

Name _____

Practice
Chapter 1
Section A

Review and Practice

(Lesson 1) Use the pictograph to answer each question.

Mail Received This Month

Letters	✉ ✉
Greeting cards	✉ ✉
Advertisements	✉ ✉ ✉ ✉
Bills	✉ ✉ ✉

✉ = 4 items of mail

1. How many letters were received? _____

2. Which type of mail was received the most? _____

3. How many symbols would there be if 20 greeting cards were received? _____

(Lesson 2) Use the bar graph to answer each question.

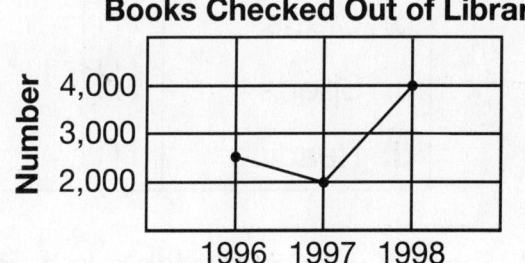

Favorite Kinds of Fruit

4. Which fruit was the least favorite? _____

5. Which fruit did 10 people vote for? _____

6. How many more voted for apples than oranges? _____

(Lesson 3) Use the line graph to answer each question.

Books Checked Out of Library

7. In what year were the most books checked out? _____

8. In what year were only 2,000 books checked out? _____

(Lesson 5) Tell which operation you would use. Then solve.

9. There are 12 boys in the class. 8 have brown eyes. How many do not have brown eyes? _____

(Mixed Review) Add or subtract.

10. 6 + 9 = _____   **11.** 8 − 6 = _____   **12.** 7 + 7 = _____

Use with page 24. **7**

Name _____

Practice 1-7

Exploring Organizing Data

1. This tally table shows students' votes for their favorite colors. Write the number of students who voted for each color.

Favorite Colors		
Color	Tally	Number
a. Blue	|||||	
b. Purple	||||| ||||	
c. Red			
d. Green	|||||	
e. Yellow	|||||		

2. Complete the tally table.

Our Favorite After-School Activities		
Activity	Tally	Number
a. Bike Riding	|||	
b. Crafts	|||||	
c. Sports	||||| ||	
d. Reading	||||	

3. Explain why a tally table is a useful way to present survey results.

_____

_____

8 Use with pages 26–27.

Name _____

Practice 1-8

Exploring Making Pictographs

Here are two different ways to show data using a pictograph.

Francie's Way

Foods We Like to Eat

Tacos	✱ ✱ ✱ ✱ ✱
Hot dogs	✱ ✱ ✱ ❋
Salad	✱ ✱
Pasta	✱

✱ = 10 votes

Chuck's Way

Foods We Like to Eat

Tacos	◉◉◉◉◉◉◉◉◉◉
Hot dogs	◉◉◉◉◉◉◉
Salad	◉◉◉◉
Pasta	◉◉

◉ = 5 votes

1. Describe one difference between the 2 pictographs.

_____

2. Students like to study in different places. Complete the pictograph. Use the data in the table.

Where Students Like to Study

Library	|||||	
At a desk	||||| ||||| |||||	
On the bed	||||| |||
On the floor	||||| |||||
Other	||||| ||||| ||

Where Students Like to Study

Library	■ ■ ■
At a desk	
On the bed	
On the floor	
Other	

■ = 2 students

3. Suppose each symbol in the pictograph above represented 3 students. How many symbols would there be for "Other"? _____

Use with pages 28–29.

Name _____

Practice 1-9

Exploring Making Bar Graphs

Here are two bar graphs that show the same data.

Brianna's Way

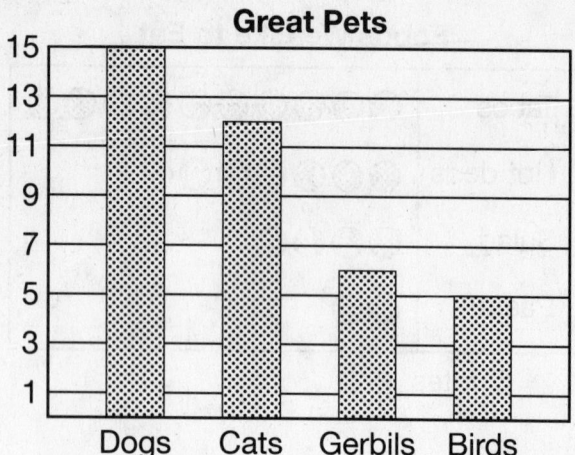

Elijah's Way

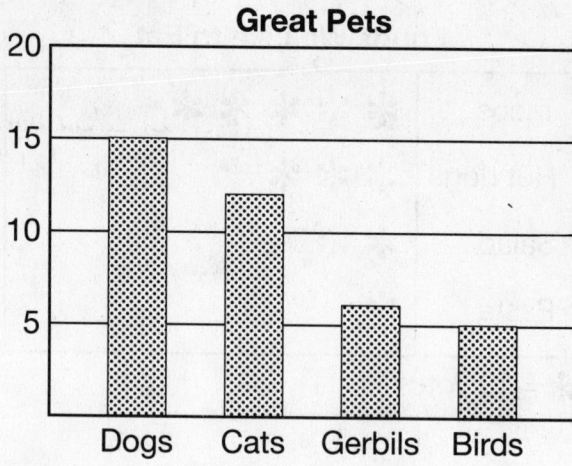

1. Describe how the bar graphs are different.

_____

Use the data in the table to complete the bar graph.

Day	Number of Books Sold
Monday	6
Tuesday	9
Wednesday	3
Thursday	12
Friday	9

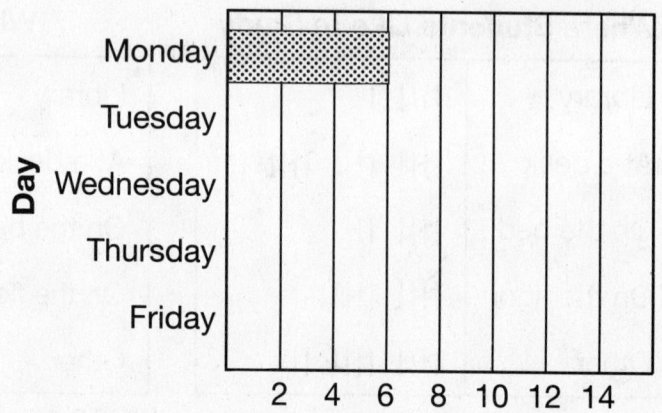

2. Complete the bar graph.

3. How many more books were sold on Tuesday than Monday? _____

4. On what days were the same number of books sold?

_____

5. How would you display this data in a pictograph?

10   Use with pages 30–31.

Name _____

Practice 1-10

Decision Making

Suppose the members of your class are collecting containers for recycling. The table shows the kind and number of containers collected.

Items Collected	
Aluminum cans	80
Milk containers	45
Soft drinks	65
Large glass	50
Small glass	15

1. Look at the data. Is the information best suited for a bar graph or a pictograph? Explain.

   _____

   _____

2. What would you title the graph?

   _____

3. Use the space provided to make a graph. If you make a pictograph, let each symbol show 10 containers. If you make a bar graph, make a scale by counting by 10s.

4. What if each symbol in your pictograph showed 5 containers? Or, what if you made your scale in your bar graph by counting by 5s? How would your graph be different?

   _____

   _____

   _____

Use with pages 32–33. **11**

Name _____

Practice
1-11

Analyze Strategies: Look for a Pattern

Look for a pattern to help you solve each problem.

1. If the pattern continues, which shape should come next? _____

 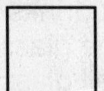    

2. If the pattern continues, which shape should come next? _____

  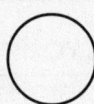  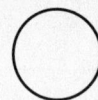 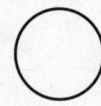 

3. What are the next 3 numbers?

   2, 6, 10, 14, _____, _____, _____

4. What are the next 3 numbers?

   10, 20, 30, 40, _____, _____, _____

5. Andrea says, "The next picture in this pattern should be a spoon." Do you agree or disagree? Explain.

_____

Look for a pattern or use any strategy to help you solve each problem.

6. Members of the Sal Pal Club receive member cards with their member I.D. number. The first member's number is 111. The second member's number is 121. The third and fourth members' numbers are 131 and 141.

   a. What I.D. numbers should be given to the next 2 members? _____

   b. What two I.D. numbers could the tenth member receive that would still fit the pattern? Explain.

_____

_____

12 Use with pages 38–41.

Name _____

Practice
Chapter 1
Section B

Review and Practice

(Lesson 7) Complete the tally table.

1. Number of pets in the homes of Mr. Gregory's third grade class:

   2, 1, 0, 2, 2, 0, 0, 1, 2, 1, 0, 0, 2, 1,

   1, 2, 0, 0, 1, 1, 1, 1, 0

Pets	Tally	Number
0		
1		
2		

(Lesson 8) Use the data in the table. Complete the pictograph.

2.

My Favorite Flavor	
Peppermint	5
Chocolate	15
Butterscotch	7

My Favorite Flavor

Peppermint	
Chocolate	
Butterscotch	

Key ⬤ = 2

(Lesson 9) Use the data in the table. Complete the bar graph.

3.

Warren's Reading Time	
Day of Week	Minutes
Monday	30
Tuesday	20
Wednesday	15
Thursday	35

(Lesson 11) Solve. Use any strategy.

4. Leandra is learning to play the trombone. She increases her practice time by 3 minutes each day. Monday she practiced 8 minutes. How many minutes will she practice on Friday? _____

(Mixed Review) Add or subtract.

5. $6 + 9 =$ _____   6. $16 - 9 =$ _____   7. $5 + 8 =$ _____

Name _____

Practice
Chapter 1

Cumulative Review

(Chapter 1 Lessons 1 and 8) Use the data to complete the pictograph.

1.

Number of Rooms in Home	
Marlene	5
Patrick	4
Lois	6

Number of Rooms in Home	
Marlene	
Patrick	
Lois	

Key: 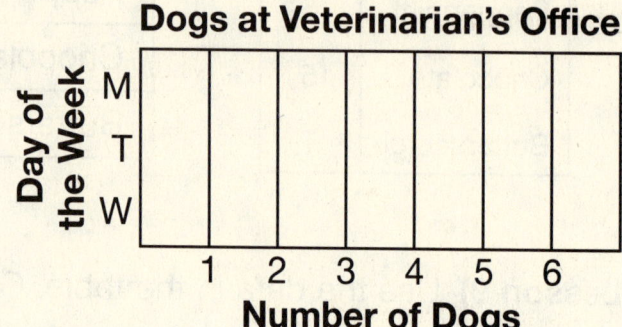 = 2 rooms

2. How many symbols would you use to represent 11 rooms? _____

(Chapter 1 Lessons 2 and 9) Use the data to complete the bar graph.

3.

Dogs at Veterinarian's Office	
Day of Week	Number of Dogs
Monday	3
Tuesday	1
Wednesday	5

4. How many dogs were seen by the veterinarian on all three days?

_____

(Chapter 1 Lesson 3) Use the line graph to answer the questions.

5. How many children played soccer in 1996?

_____

6. Do you think the number of children playing soccer in 1999 will be greater than in 1998? Explain.

_____

_____

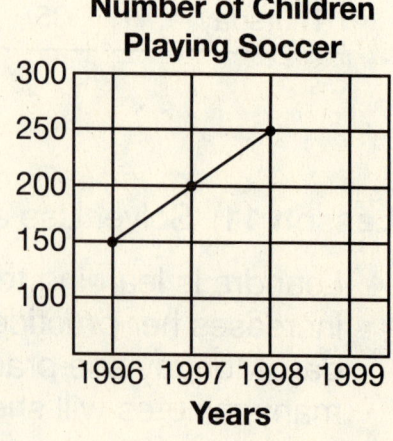

(Facts Review) Add or subtract.

7. $13 - 7 =$ _____

8. $6 + 8 =$ _____

9. $7 + 5 =$ _____

10. $7 - 4 =$ _____

14 Use with page 47.

Name _____

Practice 2-1

Place Value Through Hundreds

Write each number in standard form.

1.
2. _____

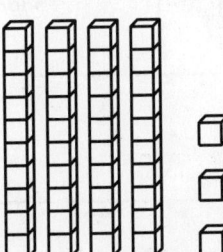 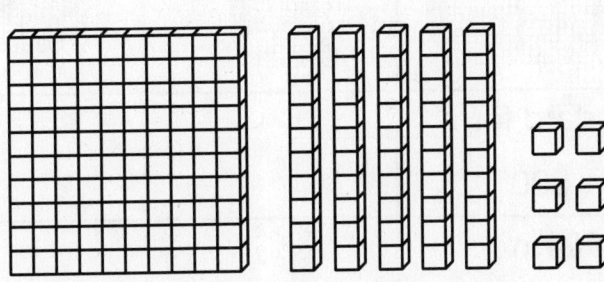

3. forty-nine _____
4. thirteen _____
5. 200 + 70 + 8 _____
6. 100 + 30 + 2 _____
7. 300 + 30 _____
8. sixty-five _____
9. 200 + 2 _____
10. 500 + 40 + 5 _____
11. two hundred sixty-two _____
12. three hundred forty-seven _____

Write the word name for each number.

13. 93 _____
14. 348 _____
15. 102 _____
16. 56 _____
17. 210 _____
18. 312 _____
19. 452 _____
20. 205 _____

21. In the number 349, which digit has the least value? Explain.

_____

22. To write the number three hundred ten, do you need a 0? Explain.

_____

23. Write the numbers five hundred ten and five hundred one.

_____

Use with pages 52–53. **15**

Name _____

Practice 2-2

Exploring Place-Value Relationships

Complete.

	[thousands blocks]	[hundred block]	[tens rods]	[ones cubes]
1.	standard form ____ , 000			
2.	word form _____ thousand			
3.	3 thousands = ____ hundreds	4 hundreds = ____ tens	16 tens = ____ hundred, ____ tens	17 ones = ____ ten, ____ ones

Write each number in standard form.

4. _____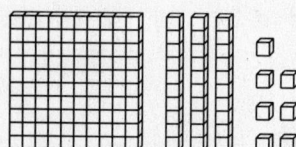

5. _____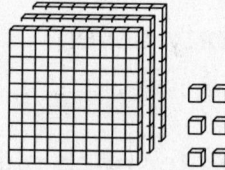

Complete the table.

	Number	Number of Ones	Number of Tens	Number of Hundreds
6.	100	100		
7.	700			7
8.	400		40	
9.	1,000	1,000		

10. How many ways can you write 600? Write them.

_____

11. How many ways can you write 5,000? Write them.

_____

16 Use with pages 54–55.

Name _____

Practice 2-3

Place Value Through Thousands

Write each number in standard form.

1. _____ 2. _____

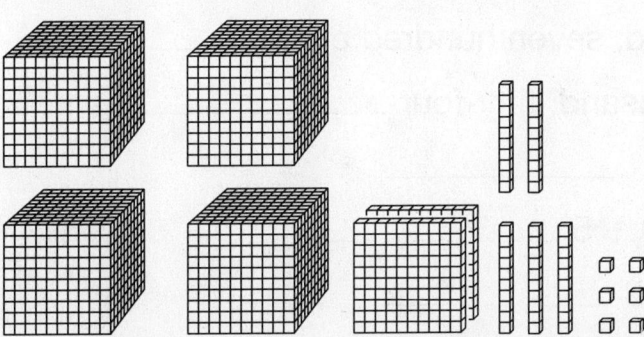 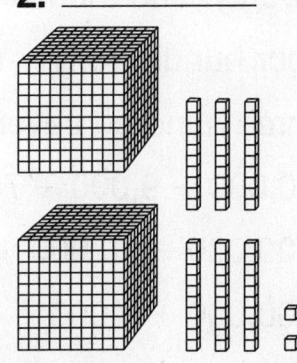

3. three thousand, four hundred seventeen _____
4. six thousand, seven hundred thirty-eight _____
5. 2,000 + 60 + 8 _____   6. 7,000 + 100 + 40 + 5 _____

Write the word name for each number.

7. 393 _____
8. 9,463 _____
9. 6,795 _____

Complete the table.

	Number	100 More	100 Less
10.	2,612		
11.	3,911		
12.	6,208		

13. Is 27 hundreds the same as 27 tens? Explain.

_____

14. Is 100 the same as 10 ones or 10 tens? _____

15. Choose a number greater than 1,000 and write it 3 ways.

_____

Use with pages 56–57.

Practice 2-4

Place Value Through Hundred Thousands

Write each number in standard form.

1. twenty-nine thousand, five hundred sixteen _____
2. four hundred thirty-five thousand, seven hundred eight _____
3. three hundred seventy-two thousand, fifty-four _____
4. 20,000 + 9,000 + 700 + 80 + 1 _____
5. 900,000 + 50,000 + 1,000 + 70 + 5 _____
6. 700,000 + 2,000 + 400 + 80 + 2 _____

Write the value of each underlined digit.

7. <u>2</u>3,045 _____
8. 5<u>6</u>2,021 _____
9. <u>8</u>03,096 _____
10. 451,3<u>8</u>2 _____
11. 12,<u>5</u>38 _____
12. 837,03<u>6</u> _____
13. 34,<u>7</u>89 _____
14. 8<u>9</u>,123 _____
15. <u>3</u>24,598 _____
16. 4<u>7</u>8,654 _____

17. Which digit has the least value in 34,187? Explain.

_____

_____

18. How many thousands is 100,000? How many ten thousands?

_____

19. Using the digits 2, 4, and 6, write a number with a 4 in the hundred thousands place and a 2 in the hundreds place.

_____

20. Using the digits 1, 3, and 5 only once, write the greatest and least three-digit numbers you can.

_____

Name _____

Practice 2-5

Analyze Strategies: Make an Organized List

Make a list or use any strategy to help solve each.

1. Suppose Carlos wants to order 40 light bulbs for the factory. He can buy light bulbs in boxes of 4 or 8. How many ways could he order exactly 40 bulbs?

    a. List all possible ways he could order 40 light bulbs.

boxes of 8						
boxes of 4						

    b. How many ways are there? _____

2. Suppose Susan wants 49 boxes of light bulbs. She can order them in packs of 10 boxes or 1 box at a time. How many ways can she order 49 boxes?

    _____
    _____
    _____

3. Pamela has a red shirt and a white shirt, black pants and a yellow skirt. How many different outfits can she make?

    _____

4. Three students are waiting in line to buy a venus fly trap. Barb is behind Jan. Mike is first in line. In what order are the students standing? _____

5. Don and Carrie had 13 orders for plants in the last two days. If they had 5 orders yesterday, how many orders did they have today? _____

6. When would you make a list to solve a problem?

    _____
    _____

Name _____

Practice
Chapter 2
Section A

Review and Practice

Vocabulary Choose the best number for each description.

_____ 1. Standard form   a. 240

_____ 2. Expanded form   b. 0, 1, 2, 3, 4, 5, 6, 7, 8, and 9

_____ 3. Digits   c. 300 + 50 + 2

(Lesson 1) Write the word name for each number.

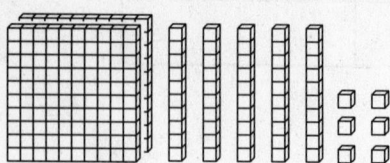 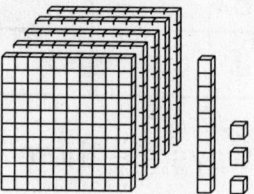

4. _____   5. _____

6. 246 _____   7. 80 + 2 _____

(Lesson 2) Write each missing value.

8. 60 ones = _____ tens   9. _____ ones = 3 hundreds
10. 70 tens = _____ hundreds   11. _____ tens = 600 ones

(Lesson 3) Write each number in standard form.

12. seven thousand three _____   13. 5,000 + 700 + 7 _____

(Lesson 4) Write the value of each underlined digit.

14. 235,641 _____   15. 899,002 _____

(Lesson 5) Make a list to help solve.

16. Kara needs $35 for an aquarium for 6 fish. How can she pay with the least ten and one dollar bills?

_____

(Mixed Review) Add or subtract.

17. 7 + 3 = _____   18. 16 − 7 = _____   19. 9 + 9 = _____

Name _____

Practice 2-6

Comparing Numbers

Compare. Use <, >, or =.

1. 27 ◯ 24
2. 416 ◯ 925
3. 2,197 ◯ 3,208
4. 2,450 ◯ 450
5. 20 ◯ 311
6. 1,717 ◯ 7,171
7. 624 ◯ 620
8. 329 ◯ 923

Write "is less than," "is greater than," or "equals."

9. 47 _____ 74

10. 1,444 _____ 1,399

11. 919 _____ 919

12. 436 _____ 4,360

13. 426 and 264 have the same digits, but in a different order. Do they have the same value? Explain.

_____

_____

14. Can you compare the 4 in 934 with the 4 in 647 to find how 934 and 647 compare? Explain.

_____

_____

Complete.

15. To compare 2,457 and 2,464 you should look at the digits in the _____ place.

16. To compare 1,830 and 1,799 you should look at the digits in the _____ place.

Use with pages 64–65

Name _____

Practice 2-7

Ordering Numbers

Order from least to greatest.

1. 649, 469, 964   _____
2. 215, 512, 255   _____
3. 375, 752, 527   _____
4. 823, 838, 282   _____
5. 439, 394, 934   _____

Order from greatest to least.

6. 315, 153, 453   _____
7. 8,042; 4,028; 2,408   _____
8. 3,962; 2,396; 9,632   _____
9. 484, 884, 448   _____
10. 1,256; 1,652; 2,165   _____

11. Circle the number that comes between 3,010 and 3,325.

    3,001   3,332   3,125   3,521

12. Circle the greatest number.

    2,909   2,999   2,990   2,900

13. Write a number between 2,458 and 3,002.

    _____

14. Write a number between 2,999 and 3,008.

    _____

Name _____

Practice 2-8

Rounding to Tens

Round to the nearest ten.

1. 47 _____   2. 14 _____   3. 25 _____
4. 42 _____   5. 38 _____   6. 16 _____
7. 111 _____   8. 105 _____   9. 674 _____
10. 417 _____ 11. 326 _____ 12. 575 _____
13. 233 _____ 14. 620 _____ 15. 337 _____
16. 517 _____ 17. 224 _____ 18. 889 _____
19. 28 _____   20. 620 _____ 21. 55 _____
22. 155 _____ 23. 8 _____   24. 404 _____

25. Joanne's bus was 27 minutes late tonight. She called to say she would be about a half hour late for dinner. Explain why this was correct.

_____

26. The library in Frank's town is 16 blocks from his house. When he asked to walk there alone, he told his mother that it was about 10 blocks away. Is this correct? Explain.

_____

27. Beth has read 218 pages of her new book. She tells a friend that to the nearest 10 she has read 210 pages. Is this correct?

_____

28. Name 3 two-digit numbers that round to 60 when rounded to the nearest ten.

_____

29. Name 3 three-digit numbers that round to 250 when rounded to the nearest ten.

_____

Name _____

Practice 2-9

Rounding to Hundreds
Round to the nearest hundred.

1. 427 _____   2. 453 _____   3. $178 _____
4. 211 _____   5. $319 _____   6. 296 _____
7. 871 _____   8. $531 _____   9. 497 _____
10. 902 _____   11. 890 _____   12. 711 _____
13. 623 _____   14. 451 _____   15. 366 _____
16. $350 _____ 17. 95 _____   18. $329 _____

19. Round 79 to the nearest hundred. _____

20. Round 152 to the nearest hundred. _____

21. Round 242 to the nearest hundred. _____

22. What is the greatest number that rounds to 700 when you round to the nearest hundred? _____

23. What is the least number that rounds to 700 when you round to the nearest hundred? _____

24. Write any 5 numbers less than 400 that round to 400 when you round to the nearest hundred.

_____

25. Write any 5 numbers greater than 400 that round to 400 when you round to the nearest hundred.

_____

26. Give the greatest and least numbers that round to 500 when rounded to the nearest 100.

_____

Use with pages 70–71.

Name _____

Practice
Chapter 2
Section B

Review and Practice

Vocabulary Match each with its definition.

_____ 1. compare   a. one way to estimate

_____ 2. round   b. to place a set of numbers from least to greatest or greatest to least

_____ 3. order   c. a way to decide which of two numbers is greater

(Lesson 6) Compare. Use <, >, or =.

4. 623 ◯ 632   5. 2,300 ◯ 320   6. 556 ◯ 655

7. 8,900 ◯ 8,900   8. 367 ◯ 1,240   9. 459 ◯ 459

(Lesson 7) Order from least to greatest.

10. 308, 299, 315 _____

11. 2,453; 2,053; 998 _____

12. 1,245; 1,425; 542 _____

Order from greatest to least.

13. 5,180; 5,108; 5,810 _____

14. 606; 6,006; 6,600 _____

(Lesson 8) Round to the nearest ten.

15. 71 _____   16. 38 _____   17. $45 _____

(Lesson 9) Round to the nearest hundred.

18. 651 _____   19. $439 _____   20. $860 _____

21. Clara found pictures of her mother dated 1978, 1971, 1983, and 1973. Clara wants to put them in order from oldest to newest. Write the dates in order. _____

(Mixed Review) Compare. Write <, >, or =.

22. 6 + 9 ◯ 9 + 6   23. 8 − 5 ◯ 7 − 2   24. 9 + 3 ◯ 15 − 4

Name _____

Practice 2-10

Time to the Nearest Five Minutes

Write each time two ways.

1.

_____
_____

2.

_____
_____

3.

_____
_____

4.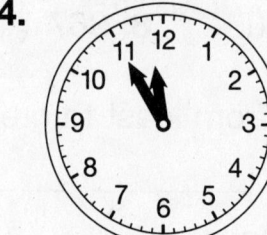

_____
_____

5.

_____
_____

6.

_____
_____

7. How many minutes are between 8:20 and 8:35? _____

8. What's another way to write 10 minutes before five? _____

9. Suppose it's 8:45. What time will it be
   15 minutes later? _____

26 Use with pages 74–75.

Name _____

Practice 2-11

Exploring Time to the Nearest Minute

Write each time two ways.

1.

   _____

2.

   _____

3.

   _____

4.

   _____

5.

   _____

6.

   _____

7. Duke's vet appointment is at 4:30. You arrive at 4:17. Are you early or late?

   _____

8. If it is 3:22, in how many minutes will it be 3:30?

   _____

9. Suppose you waited 12 minutes for your school bus. About how many minutes did you wait? Round to the nearest ten minutes.

   _____

Use with pages 76–77.

Name _____

Practice 2-12

Time to the Half Hour and Quarter Hour

Write each time two ways. Write A.M. or P.M.

1.  go to a Saturday afternoon movie

_____

_____

2.  sunrise

_____

_____

3.  school's out

_____

_____

4.  sleep time

_____

_____

5.  dinner time

_____

_____

6.  lunch time

_____

_____

7. Write a time that is between noon and half past twelve in the afternoon. _____

8. Write a time that is between quarter to three and quarter after three in the morning. _____

9. How many times in one day will the clock show 6:30? Explain. _____

Name _____

Practice 2-13

Elapsed Time

1. Sam wants to let his dog run for twenty minutes. If he starts at 12:15 P.M., what time should he call the dog in? _____

2. "I tried to call you an hour ago!" says Sheila. If it is 8:45 P.M. now, what time did she call before? _____

3. "This movie lasts for 2 hours and 45 minutes," says Marc. If it begins at 7:00 P.M., what time will the movie end? _____

4. Kai started his homework at 4:35 P.M. and finished at 7:00 P.M. How much time did he spend doing homework? _____

5. Carla's karate class lasts for 45 minutes. If it begins at 4:15 P.M., what time will it end? _____

6. Suppose it is 6:20 A.M. What time will it be in half an hour? _____

7. The school bus arrives at 7:15 A.M. It is now 6:35 A.M. How much time does Amir have to get ready? _____

Three cars left school at 2:30 P.M. Each traveled for the amount of time shown. When did each car arrive at its destination?

Car	Driving Time	Arrival Time
8. Juan's car	35 minutes	_____
9. Hannah's car	60 minutes	_____
10. Beryl's car	1 hour and 5 minutes	_____

Use with pages 80–81. **29**

Name _____

Practice 2-14

Ordinal Numbers and the Calendar
Use the calendar to answer 1–6.

February

Sun.	Mon.	Tues.	Wed.	Thur.	Fri.	Sat.
				1	2	3
4	5	6	7	8	9	10
11	12	13	14	15	16	17
18	19	20	21	22	23	24
25	26	27	28			

1. How many Tuesdays are in this month? _____

2. Abraham Lincoln was born on February 12th.
   What day of the week is that? _____
   Mark it on the calendar above.

3. George Washington was born on the twenty-second of February.
   What day of the week is that? _____
   Mark it on the calendar above.

4. What day of the week is February 3rd? _____

5. What is the date of the third Saturday in February?
   _____

6. What are the dates of the last weekend in February?
   _____

7. February is the second month of the year. What is the first month?
   _____

8. Name the fourth month. _____

30 Use with pages 82–83.

Name _____

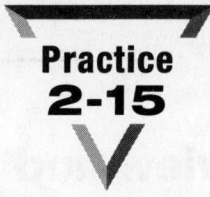

Practice
2-15

Decision Making

1. Part of making a schedule is knowing how much time you have to get everything done. Figure out how much time you have available for each activity on this list and write it down.

   Activity **Total time**

   a. The meeting begins at 3:15 P.M.
   and lasts until 4:00 P.M. _____

   b. You have from 6:00 P.M. until
   8:20 P.M. to do your homework. _____

   c. Practice begins at 3:45 P.M. and
   ends at 5:15 P.M. _____

   d. You begin your chores at 8:30 A.M.
   and must be done by noon. _____

2. Another step in making a schedule is estimating—or guessing—how long something will take. Give it a try. Estimate how long it would take you to:

   a. brush your teeth _____

   b. clean your room _____

   c. read 10 pages _____

   d. play a game of checkers _____

   e. walk to the nearest store _____

   f. make a sandwich _____

   g. change your clothes _____

   h. take a bath _____

Use with pages 84–85. **31**

Name _____

Practice
Chapter 2
Section C

Review and Practice

Vocabulary Match each word with its definition.

_____ 1. A.M.   a. times from noon to midnight

_____ 2. P.M.   b. numbers used for ordering

_____ 3. ordinal numbers   c. times from midnight to noon

(Lessons 10, 11, and 12) Write each time two ways. Write A.M. or P.M.

4.
after lunch

_____

_____

5.
prepare dinner

_____

_____

6.
get dressed

_____

_____

(Lesson 13) Write each time.

7. Daniela ate lunch at 12:30 P.M. and went fishing 2 hours and 15 minutes later. What time did she go fishing? _____

8. Justin began his chores at 9 A.M. and ended at 11:15 A.M. How long was he doing his chores? _____

(Lesson 14) Use the calendar to answer 9 and 10.

9. What day of the week is the 23rd?

_____

10. How many Mondays are in the month shown?

_____

October

Sun.	Mon.	Tues.	Wed.	Thur.	Fri.	Sat.
				1	2	3
4	5	6	7	8	9	10
11	12	13	14	15	16	17
18	19	20	21	22	23	24
25	26	27	28	29	30	31

(Mixed Review) Write the value of each digit in 473,826.

11. 8 _____   12. 4 _____

13. 7 _____

Use with page 86.

Name _____

Practice
Chapters 1–2

Cumulative Review

(Chapter 1 Lesson 2) Use the data from the graph to answer each question.

1. How many sports are the favorite of more than 5 students? _____

2. What sport is the favorite of 9 students? _____

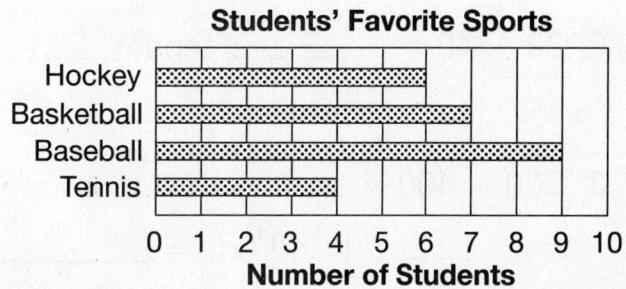

(Chapter 1 Lesson 5) Write a number sentence and use it to solve the problem.

3. Liz read 10 books. 6 were mysteries. The rest were biographies. How many were biographies? _____

(Chapter 1 Lesson 11) Write the next four numbers.

4. 10, 20, 30, 40, _____, _____, _____, _____

5. 29, 26, 23, 20, _____, _____, _____, _____

(Chapter 2 Lesson 4) Write the value of each underlined digit.

6. 64<u>5</u>,861 _____   7. 293,<u>8</u>62 _____

(Chapter 2 Lesson 7) Order from least to greatest.

8. 455, 450, 530, 545 _____

9. 4,670, 5,839, 4,668, 5,355 _____

(Chapter 2 Lesson 10) Write each time in two ways.

10.

11.

_____   _____

Use with page 91. **33**

Name _____

Practice 3-1

Exploring Addition Patterns

Use basic facts and place value to complete each problem.

1. 3 + 4 = _____

2. 30 + 40 = _____ tens + _____ tens
   = _____ tens = _____

3. 300 + 400 = _____ hundreds + _____ hundreds
   = _____ hundreds = _____

4. 3 + 5 = _____
   30 + _____ = 80
   _____ + 500 = 800

5. 4 + 9 = _____
   _____ + 90 = 130
   400 + _____ = 1,300

6. 8 + 1 = _____
   80 + _____ = 90
   _____ + 100 = 900

7. 8 + 7 = _____
   _____ + 70 = 150
   800 + _____ = 1,500

Find each sum using mental math.

8. $20 + $50 = _____

9. 100 + 700 = _____

10. 600 + 400 = _____

11. $30 + $80 = _____

12. 20 + 90 = _____

13. $60 + $70 = _____

14. There are 30 students on one school bus and 70 on another school bus. How many students are there altogether? _____

15. Can you use the basic fact 3 + 2 to add 30 + 200? Explain.
    _____
    _____

34 Use with pages 96–97.

Name _____

Practice 3-2

Exploring Adding on a Hundred Chart

You can think about adding numbers in different ways.

1. 50 + 36 = 50 + 30 + _____ = _____

Show how you can use the hundred chart to add 48 and 37.

2. 48 + 37 = _____

1	2	3	4	5	6	7	8	9	10
11	12	13	14	15	16	17	18	19	20
21	22	23	24	25	26	27	28	29	30
31	32	33	34	35	36	37	38	39	40
41	42	43	44	45	46	47	48	49	50
51	52	53	54	55	56	57	58	59	60
61	62	63	64	65	66	67	68	69	70
71	72	73	74	75	76	77	78	79	80
81	82	83	84	85	86	87	88	89	90
91	92	93	94	95	96	97	98	99	100

Find each sum. You may use the hundred chart to help.

3. 43 + 20 = _____
4. 52 + 18 = _____
5. 27 + 6 = _____
6. 6 + 27 = _____
7. $78 + $21 = _____
8. 40 + 45 = _____
9. 37 + 14 = _____
10. $13 + $29 = _____

11. Find the sum of 14 and 67. _____

12. Add 54 and 39. _____

13. If you know the sum of 24 + 37, how can you find the sum of 37 + 24? Explain.

_____

_____

14. Explain how you would add 39 + 22 using mental math.

_____

Use with pages 98–99.

Name _____

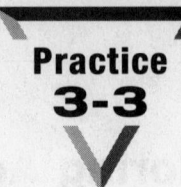

Exploring Algebra: Missing Numbers

There are two ways to find the missing number in ☐ + 4 = 21.

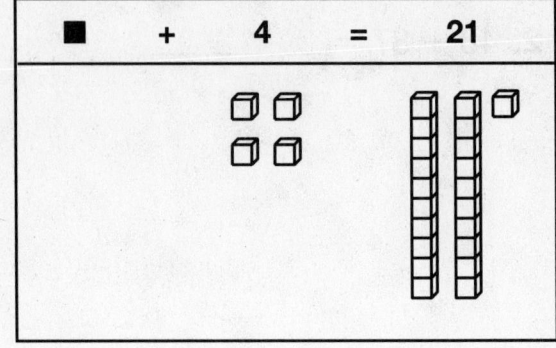

1. Match 4 cubes on one side with 4 on the other. How many more cubes do you need to make 21?

    _____ + 4 = 21.

2. You already have 4 on one side, so you can count on from 4 until you have 21.

    You count on _____ more cubes.

Find each missing number. You may use color cubes to help.

3. _____ + 7 = 23   4. _____ + 8 = 14   5. _____ + 5 = 12

6. _____ + 6 = 21   7. 4 + _____ = 10   8. 9 + _____ = 28

9. 11 + _____ = 19   10. _____ + 13 = 22   11. _____ + 19 = 23

12. Is the missing number in ☐ + 4 = 16 the same as the missing number in 4 + ☐ = 16? Explain.

    _____

    _____

Use patterns to find each missing number.

13. _____ + 7 = 13   14. 6 + _____ = 13   15. _____ + 5 = 11

16. 6 + _____ = 11   17. 3 + _____ = 12   18. _____ + 9 = 12

Name _____

Practice 3-4

Estimating Sums

Estimate each sum.

1. 48 + 39 _____

2. 713 + 224 _____

3. $354 + $239 _____

4. $77 + $62 _____

5. 85 + 41 _____

6. 528 + 867 _____

7. 91 + 26 _____

8. 333 + 690 _____

9. Estimate the sum of 915 and 166. _____

10. Estimate the sum of 43 and 25. _____

11. Estimate the sum of $67 and $62. _____

12. Two addends have a sum of about 800. What are two possible addends?

_____

13. Two addends have a sum of about 70. What are two possible addends?

_____

14. Round to find which two pairs of numbers have a sum of about 700.

    412   355   268   508   149

_____

15. Round to estimate the sum of all the numbers in 14.

_____

Name _____

Practice
Chapter 3
Section A

Review and Practice

Vocabulary Match each with its definition.

_____ 1. estimate   a. the answer obtained when adding numbers

_____ 2. sum   b. to find an answer that is close to an exact answer

(Lesson 1) Complete.

3. 8 + 8 = _____

   80 + _____ = 160

   _____ + 800 = 1,600

4. $3 + $_____ = $12

   $_____ + $90 = $120

   $300 + $900 = $_____

5. What basic fact can you use to find 300 + 800? _____

(Lesson 2) Find each sum. You may use a hundred chart to help.

6. 36 + 8 = _____

7. 82 + 12 = _____

8. 25 + 30 = _____

9. $64 + $27 = _____

(Lesson 3) Find each missing number. You may use color cubes to help.

10. _____ + 7 = 32

11. 8 + _____ = 30

12. I am a 2-digit number. If you add me to 6 you will get a sum of 38. What number am I? _____

(Lesson 4) Circle the letter that shows the best estimate of each sum.

13. 34 + 55   a. 80   b. 100   c. 90

14. 522 + 131   a. 600   b. 700   c. 800

(Mixed Review) Use the pictograph to answer each question.

15. How many students does each 🐱 represent? _____

16. How many boys have cats? _____

17. How many more girls than boys have cats? _____

38 Use with page 104.

Name _____

Practice 3-5

Exploring Adding with Regrouping

Find each sum. You may use place-value blocks to help.

1. 24 + 47

    a. How many ones? _____
    b. Do you need to regroup? _____
    c. How many tens? _____
    d. Do you need to regroup? _____
    e. 24 + 47 = _____

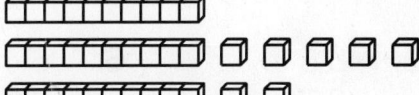

2. 18 + 55 = _____   3. 34 + 28 = _____

4. 62 + 43 = _____   5. 59 + 21 = _____

6. 77 + 69 = _____   7. 45 + 86 = _____

8. 32 + 39 = _____   9. 29 + 99 = _____

10. 33 + 57 = _____   11. 62 + 39 = _____

12. 58 + 46 = _____   13. 16 + 86 = _____

14. 89 + 75 = _____   15. 57 + 24 = _____

16. 35 + 97 = _____   17. 59 + 79 = _____

18. Do you need to regroup 10 ones for 1 ten when you add 56 + 37? Explain.

_____

19. Do you need to regroup 10 ones for 1 ten when you add 56 + 42? Explain.

_____

Use with pages 106–107.

Name _____

Practice 3-6

Adding 2-Digit Numbers

Add. Estimate to check.

1. 43
   +16

2. 26
   +72

3. $39
   +41

4. 52
   + 9

5. 85
   +67

6. 64
   +89

7. 96
   + 6

8. $58
   +15

9. 22
   +81

10. $54
    + 7

11. 88
    +99

12. 16
    +77

13. 91
    +79

14. 76
    +37

15. 55
    +86

16. 47
    +65

17. 28 + 54 = _____

18. $37 + $78 = _____

19. 63 + 87 = _____

20. 92 + 21 = _____

21. Find the sum of 45 and 37. _____

22. Add 38 and 19. _____

23. Write two numbers that add to 70 without regrouping.

    _____

24. When you add 27 + 5 do you start by adding 2 + 5? Explain.

    _____

40 Use with pages 108–109.

Name _____

Practice 3-7

Adding 3-Digit Numbers
Complete.

1. ²¹¹217
    + 384
    ─────
    ☐ 0 1

2. ¹583
    + 74
    ─────
    6 ☐ ☐

3. ¹¹$357
    +   66
    ─────
    ☐ 2 ☐

4. ¹445
    + 208
    ─────
    ☐ ☐ ☐

Add. Estimate to check.

5. $826
    + 151

6. 737
    +217

7. $42
    + 59

8. 431
    + 94

9. 621
    +377

10. 456
    +255

11. 388
    + 94

12. $982
    + 635

13. 97 + 42 = _____

14. 358 + 715 = _____

15. $39 + $75 = _____

16. 118 + 647 = _____

17. Find the sum of 380 and 442.

18. Find the sum of 832 and 79.

19. Write two addends with a sum of 258.

_____

20. Estimate to decide which sum is greater than 1,000:
    590 + 462 or 311 + 628.

_____

Use with pages 110–113.

Name _____

Practice 3-8

Adding 4-Digit Numbers: Choose a Calculation Method

Add.

1. 5,347
  +2,491

2. 6,200
  +3,500

3. 4,619
  +1,592

4. 7,416
  +2,347

5. $2,400
  +5,500

6. 1,348
  + 721

7. 4,827
  +3,164

8. 6,038
  + 831

9. 6,371
  +2,293

10. 3,849
  +5,163

11. 7,345
  +1,681

12. 4,691
  +5,366

13. 1,495 + 5,622 = _____

14. 6,400 + 3,500 = _____

15. 9,046 + 716 = _____

16. $5,807 + $2,164 = _____

17. Find the sum of 648 and 2,115.
   _____

18. Find the sum of 2,800 and 5,000.
   _____

19. Estimate to decide if the sum of 6,701 and 2,399 is greater than or less than 10,000.

   _____

20. Which two numbers have a sum of 6,000?

   1,500   5,000   3,000
   2,000   4,500   3,500

   _____

42 Use with pages 116–117.

Name _____

Practice 3-9

Column Addition
Add.

1.   78
       94
    +   5

2.   416
      172
    + 21

3.   660
      218
    + 34

4.   54
      793
    + 415

5.   348
      506
    + 270

6.   529
       32
    + 410

7.   481
        9
    + 573

8.   855
       26
    + 91

9. 84 + 394 + 250 = _____

10. 15 + 7 + 989 = _____

11. What is the sum of 23, 462, and 117?

    _____

12. Add 851, 756, and 922.

    _____

13. What is the greatest possible sum using three of these numbers?

    | 97 | 541 | 472 | 149 | 608 |

    _____

14. To add 67 + 45 + 821, would you start by adding 6 + 4 + 2? Why or why not?

    _____

    _____

15. Does it matter in which order you write 549, 192, 420 and 37 to add?

    _____

Name _____

Practice 3-10

Analyze Strategies: Guess and Check

Guess and check to solve.

1. The Hawks beat the Jays in a baseball game. The scores were 6 runs apart and there were 22 runs scored in the game. How many runs did each team score?

   _____

2. The Hawks lost to the Orioles by 4 runs. There were 18 runs scored in the game. How many runs did the Orioles score?

   _____

Use any strategy to solve.

3. The Jays beat the Orioles by 8 runs. There were 16 runs scored in the game. How many runs did the Jays score?

   _____

4. The sum of two numbers is 65. The numbers are 3 apart. What are they?

   _____

5. The sum of two numbers is 92. The numbers are 12 apart. What are they?

   _____

6. Tim bought three items at the school bookstore. He spent $23. What did Tim buy? Use the prices in the table to solve.

Item	Cost
Backpack	$14
Calculator	$ 9
Dictionary	$ 5
Notebook	$ 3
Set of Markers	$ 4

_____

_____

Name _____

Practice
Chapter 3
Section B

Review and Practice

(Lesson 5) Find each sum. You may use place-value blocks to help.

1. 68 + 35 = _____
2. 237 + 125 = _____
3. 56 + 39 = _____
4. 53 + 34 = _____

(Lessons 6 and 7) Add. Estimate to check.

5. 43
   +24

6. 651
   + 86

7. 738
   +339

8. 49
   +71

9. 823 + 119 = _____
10. 545 + 126 = _____

11. Do you need to regroup 10 tens for 1 hundred when you add 241 + 387? _____

(Lessons 8 and 9) Add.

12. 2,568
   + 812

13. 355
        51
    + 19

14. 402
     313
    + 66

15. 7,220
   + 867

(Lesson 10) Guess and check to solve.

16. The Jays beat the Tigers by 5 runs. There were 17 runs scored. How many runs did the Jays score? _____

(Mixed Review) Circle the letter that answers each question.

17. Which does not tell the correct time?

   A. half after 5   **B.** 15 minutes before 5
   C. 4:45   **D.** 45 minutes after 4

18. What time will it be in 1 and a half hours?

   A. 4:15   **B.** 6:00   **C.** 6:15   **D.** 7:30

19. Sal's soccer practice began at 2:45 P.M. and finished at 4:00 P.M. How long was practice?

Name _____

Practice 3-11

Mental Math

Use mental math to find each sum.

1. 80 + 55 = _____
2. 62 + 9 = _____
3. 18 + 40 = _____
4. 45 + 35 = _____
5. 59 + 36 = _____
6. 21 + 18 = _____
7. 99 + 5 = _____
8. 73 + 9 = _____
9. 47 + 29 = _____
10. 25 + 60 = _____
11. 88 + 4 = _____
12. 7 + 43 = _____
13. 81 + 9 = _____
14. 27 + 62 = _____
15. 7 + 19 = _____
16. 32 + 21 = _____
17. 55 + 35 = _____
18. 28 + 83 = _____
19. 46 + 52 = _____
20. 67 + 9 = _____
21. 34 + 28 = _____
22. 35 + 17 = _____
23. 8 + 37 = _____
24. 42 + 17 = _____

25. Find the sum of 475 and 15.

    _____

26. Find the sum of 133 and 7.

    _____

27. Add 389 + 4.

    _____

28. Add 225 + 25.

    _____

29. How does knowing 7 + 3 = 10 help you to add 37 + 13 mentally?

    _____

    _____

30. How can finding digits that add up to 10 help you to add 64 + 26?

    _____

    _____

Use with pages 124–125.

Name _____

Practice 3-12

Counting Coins

Write the total value in cents.

1. (dime, dime, dime, dime, nickel, nickel, nickel, penny, penny)

   _____

2. (quarter, quarter, quarter, quarter, penny, penny, penny, penny)

   _____

3. (nickel, nickel, nickel, quarter, penny)

   _____

4. (dime, dime, dime, dime, dime, quarter, penny, penny, penny, nickel)

   _____

5. (half-dollar, quarter, dime)

   _____

6. (dime, dime, dime, dime, dime, nickel, nickel, nickel)

   _____

7. Find three ways to make 67 cents.

   _____

   _____

   _____

8. Find a way to make 56 cents.

   _____

9. Use the fewest coins to make 37 cents.

   _____

Use with pages 126–127. **47**

Name _____

Practice
3-13

Using Dollars and Cents

Write the total value in dollars and cents.

1.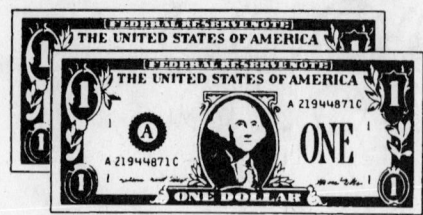

_____

2.

_____

3. Give at least two ways to show $2.65.

_____

_____

_____

_____

4. Give at least three ways to show $8.57.

_____

_____

_____

_____

_____

5. Alicia said, "I lost a coin! I had $6.96. Now I only have 1 five-dollar bill, 1 one-dollar bill, 3 quarters, 1 dime, 1 nickel, and 1 penny." What coin did Alicia lose?

_____

Name _____

Practice 3-14

Exploring Making Change

Your class is having an art sale to make money for new supplies. You are the cashier.

1. Andy buys a papier-maché mask worth $3.24. He pays with $5.00. How much change will you give him?

    a. Count on by circling the coins and bills you will use to make change. Write the amount.

    _____ _____ _____ _____ _____

    b. How much change is that? _____

2. June buys a painting worth $3.31. She pays with $5.00. List which coins and bills you would use to make change. Then write the change in dollars and cents.

    _____

    _____

3. Sheila's purchases total $2.09. She pays with $3.00.

    a. Write three ways you could make change.

    _____

    _____

    _____

    b. Which way uses the fewest coins?

    _____

Use with pages 130–131.

Name _____

Practice 3-15

Adding Money

Add. Estimate to check.

1. $5.17
   + 4.39

2. $8.89
   + 3.14

3. $0.52
   + 7.93

4. $2.22
   + 3.33

5. $4.87
   + 5.14

6. $2.06
   + 7.34

7. $9.40
   + 1.61

8. $6.73
   + 2.99

9. $4.34 + $3.71 = _____

10. $9.49 + $8.84 = _____

11. $3.25 + $2.96 = _____

12. $7.69 + $5.91 = _____

13. Find the sum of $2.41 and $5.57. _____

14. Add $8.12 + $8.69. _____

15. Will $10.00 be enough to buy a softball and a baseball bat? Explain.

   _____

16. Which two pieces of equipment together will cost about $11.00?

   _____

Athletic Equipment	
baseball bat	$7.07
basketball	$6.49
volleyball	$3.34
softball	$2.98
soccer ball	$4.63

17. What two items together would cost less than $7.00? How much would they cost?

   _____

50 Use with pages 134–135.

Name _____

Practice 3-16

Front-End Estimation

Use front-end estimation to estimate each sum.

1. $6.12
 + 3.77

2. 334
 865
 +202

3. 789
 122
 +960

4. $2.57
 5.16
 + 8.45

5. 691
 423
 +606

6. 928
 +890

7. $3.33
 5.87
 + 6.63

8. 478
 150
 +822

9. 345 + 312 + 637 _____

10. 841 + 797 + 141 _____

11. Use front-end estimation to estimate the sum of 263, 804, and 469.

12. Use front-end estimation to estimate the sum of $7.34, $3.69, and $9.51.

13. Is the sum of $4.32 + $6.90 + $7.86 greater than $17.00? Explain.

14. If you buy 2 items that cost $6.32 each, will $11.00 be enough to buy both items? Explain.

15. If you buy 3 items that cost $5.43 each, will $15.00 be enough to buy all 3 items? Explain.

16. If you buy 2 items for $6.29 and 1 item for $3.55, will $15.00 be enough? Explain.

Name _____

Practice 3-17

Analyze Word Problems: Exact Answer or Estimate?

Ahmed is going shopping for art supplies.

Art Supplies	
crayons	$2.34
marker	$4.98
paintbrush	$1.86
construction paper	$3.15
watercolor paint set	$4.43
frame	$6.71

Write if you need an exact answer or an estimate. Then solve.

1. Ahmed has a $10 bill. Does he have enough money to buy construction paper and a frame? Explain.

   _____

2. How much would it cost to buy crayons, a marker, and construction paper?

   _____

3. If Ahmed has $8.00, and he buys 3 paint brushes, does he have enough money left to buy a watercolor paint set? Explain.

   _____
   _____
   _____

4. Ahmed wants to know if $9.00 is enough to buy 2 markers. Does he need to find the exact total? Explain.

   _____

5. Ahmed began shopping at 11:30 A.M. When he finished it was 12:15 P.M. How long did he spend shopping?

   _____

Use with pages 138–139.

Name _____

Practice
Chapter 3
Section C

Review and Practice

(Lesson 11) Use mental math to find each sum.

1. 75 + 9 _____   2. 29 + 43 _____   3. 88 + 5 _____

(Lessons 12 and 13) Write the total value in cents or dollars and cents.

4.

5.

_____   _____

(Lesson 14) List which coins and bills you would use to make change. Then write the change in dollars and cents.

6. Metta buys a notebook that costs $1.19. She pays with $2.00.

_____

(Lesson 15) Add. Estimate to check.

7. $9.15 + $4.82 _____   8. $3.56 + $6.89 _____

9. $1.75 + $9.10 _____   10. $7.29 + $0.54 _____

(Lesson 16) Use front-end estimation to estimate each sum.

11. 325 + 176 + 852 _____   12. 63 + 55 + 38 _____

(Lesson 17) Write if you need an exact answer or an estimate. Then solve.

13. Cheryl wants to buy three books that cost $5.95, $2.95, and $3.45. Will $10 be enough money? Explain.

_____

_____

(Mixed Review) Write the value of each underlined number.

14. <u>4</u>5,886 _____   15. 2,84<u>6</u> _____   16. <u>1</u>23,654 _____

Use with page 140.

Name _____

Practice
Chapters 1–3

Cumulative Review
(Chapter 1, Lesson 1)

1. Which of the following uses pictures to represent information in a graph?

   A. line graph **B.** bar graph **C.** pictograph

   _____

(Chapter 1, Lesson 3)

2. Which of the following shows changes over time?

   A. line graph **B.** bar graph **C.** pictograph

   _____

(Chapter 2, Lesson 4) Write the standard form of each number.

3. four hundred thousand, sixty-seven _____

4. six hundred twenty-one thousand, one hundred ten _____

5. one hundred thirty thousand, six _____

(Chapter 2, Lesson 9) Round each to the nearest hundred.

6. 2,610   7. 987   8. 1,651   9. 705

   _____   _____   _____   _____

(Chapter 3, Lessons 9 and 15) Add.

10.   456   11.   321   12. $3.15   13. $5.11
      238   56   + 1.49   + 7.52
    + 115   + 135   _____   _____
    _____   _____

(Chapter 3, Lesson 12)

14. Dimitrios has a five-dollar bill, 2 one-dollar bills, 3 quarters, 1 dime and 2 nickels. How much money does he have?

    _____

54 Use with pages 145.

Name _____

Practice 4-1

Reviewing the Meaning of Subtraction

Write a number sentence for each. Then solve.

1. A clown is juggling four bananas. He drops one of them. How many bananas are still in the air?

   _____

2. Karen invites eight friends to her home for a party. Three people cannot come. How many people are there for the party?

   _____

3. Josh had a spelling test today. There were fifteen questions on the test. Josh misspelled six words. How many did he spell correctly?

   _____

4. Twelve children attended Melissa's party. There were seven boys. How many girls were there?

   _____

5. The bus stops and six children get on. Now there are thirteen children on the bus. How many children were on the bus before this stop?

   _____

6. The cracker box contained eighteen crackers. Now there are only nine. How many crackers were taken?

   _____

7. Jennifer has read 4 chapters of her book. The book has 16 chapters. How many chapters does she have left to read?

   _____

8. Phil has $10. He buys a vase for $6. How much money does he have left?

   _____

Name _____

Practice 4-2

Exploring Subtraction Patterns

Complete.

1. 8 − 3 = _____
   _____ − 30 = 50
   800 − _____ = 500

2. 13 − _____ = 9
   130 − 40 = _____
   _____ − 400 = 900

3. $19 − $7 = _____
   $190 − _____ = $120
   _____ − $700 = $1,200

4. 12 − 6 = _____
   _____ − 60 = 60
   _____ − 600 = 600

Find each difference using mental math.

5. 90 − 50 = _____

6. $100 − $80 = _____

7. 1,800 − 400 = _____

8. $1,200 − $1,100 = _____

9. 1,700 − 500 = _____

10. $1,100 − $600 = _____

11. Karima and Rick are playing a game with play money. Rick has $1,100. He lands on a space that makes him pay Karima $400. How much money will he have left? _____

12. Marty and Dee live in the same town. Marty's grandparents live 30 miles away. Dee's grandparents live 80 miles away. How much farther away do Dee's grandparents live? _____

13. Continue the pattern. Then write the rule.

In	70	80	90	100	110	120
Out	40	50	60			

Rule: _____

14. What basic fact could you use to find 1,300 − 500? Solve.

_____

56 Use with pages 152–153.

Name _____

Practice 4-3

Exploring Subtracting on a Hundred Chart

Find each difference. You may use a hundred chart to help.

1. 92 − 27 = _____
2. 69 − 16 = _____
3. 29 − 12 = _____
4. $77 − $64 = _____
5. 44 − 11 = _____
6. 54 − 37 = _____

Use mental math to find each difference.

7. 71 − 51 = _____
8. $48 − $20 = _____
9. 80 − 40 = _____
10. $45 − $30 = _____
11. 42 − 22 = _____
12. 51 − 21 = _____
13. 31 − 8 = _____
14. 79 − 44 = _____

Find each missing number. You may use a hundred chart to help.

15. 56 − _____ = 21
16. 32 − _____ = 7
17. _____ − 12 = 49
18. _____ − 34 = 62
19. 88 − _____ = 71
20. 89 − _____ = 61

21. On a hundred chart, Lesley begins with her finger on 89. She moves back 5 rows and back 7 spaces.

    a. On what number does she land? _____

    b. What number did she subtract? _____

22. Victor has 40¢. He wants to buy 3 postcards. Each postcard costs 20¢. How much more money will he need to buy the postcards? _____

Use with pages 154–155. **57**

Name _____

Practice 4-4

Estimating Differences

Estimate each difference.

1. 988 − 112 = _____
2. 992 − 400 = _____
3. 25 − 14 = _____
4. 98 − 22 = _____
5. 112 − 56 = _____
6. 506 − 210 = _____
7. 279 − 126 = _____
8. 767 − 547 = _____
9. $4.99 − $3.67 = _____
10. $8.22 − $4.83 = _____
11. $6.49 − $1.25 = _____
12. $5.81 − $2.84 = _____
13. 432 − 121 = _____
14. 890 − 160 = _____
15. 62 − 19 = _____
16. 81 − 76 = _____

17. Suppose the length of a movie you plan to watch is 98 minutes. You have been watching it for 50 minutes. Would it make sense to say that you have watched about half of the movie? Explain.

_____

_____

18. Suppose the book that you're reading has 126 pages. You've read 62 pages. Would it make sense to say that you have read about half of the book? Explain.

_____

19. The estimated difference of the cost of two games is $2.00. Give two examples of the exact amounts that would make the estimate reasonable.

_____

_____

20. The estimated difference of the weight of two elephants is 100 pounds. Give two examples of the exact amounts that would make the estimate reasonable.

_____

Name _____

Practice 4-5

Exploring Regrouping

Regroup 1 ten for 10 ones. You may use place-value blocks or draw a picture to help.

1. 64 is the same as _____

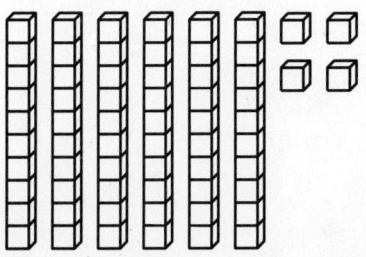

2. 42 = 3 tens, _____ ones   **3.** 95 = 8 tens, _____ ones

4. 63 = 5 tens, _____ ones   **5.** 57 = 4 tens, _____ ones

6. 53 = 4 tens, _____ ones   **7.** _____ = 5 tens, 17 ones

8. 32 = _____ tens, 12 ones   **9.** 90 = 8 tens, _____ ones

10. _____ = 3 tens, 11 ones   **11.** 88 = _____ tens, 18 ones

Regroup 1 hundred for 10 tens. You may use place-value blocks or draw a picture to help.

12. 215 = 1 hundred, _____ tens, 5 ones

13. 829 = 7 hundreds, _____ tens, 9 ones

14. 982 = 8 hundreds, _____ tens, 2 ones

15. 302 = 2 hundreds, _____ tens, 2 ones

16. 786 = 6 hundreds, _____ tens, 6 ones

17. 614 = 5 hundreds, _____ tens, 4 ones

18. Regroup 1 ten for 10 ones in the number 567.

_____

19. Regroup 1 hundred for 10 tens in the number 412.

_____

Use with pages 158–159.

Name _____

Practice
Chapter 4
Section A

Review and Practice

(Lesson 1) Write a number sentence for each. Then solve.

1. Harold bought 5 souvenirs in Maine and 3 in Massachusetts. How many more souvenirs did he buy in Maine than Massachusetts? _____

2. Phylis took 18 pictures. 9 are of the Grand Canyon. How many pictures are not of the Grand Canyon? _____

(Lesson 2) Look for a pattern. Complete.

3. $6 - 2 =$ _____
   $60 -$ _____ $= 40$
   _____ $- 200 = 400$

4. $13 -$ _____ $= 4$
   $130 - 90 =$ _____
   _____ $- 900 = 400$

5. $17 - 8 =$ _____
   $170 -$ _____ $= 90$
   $1{,}700 - 800 =$ _____

(Lesson 3) Solve. You may use a hundred chart to help.

6. $35 - 5 =$ _____

7. $\$73 - \$30 =$ _____

8. $83 - 64 =$ _____

9. $59 - 17 =$ _____

10. _____ $- 45 = 55$

11. _____ $- 28 = 16$

(Lesson 4) Estimate each difference.

12. $623 - 455$ _____

13. $\$3.75 - \$2.29$ _____

14. Suppose a movie lasts 100 minutes. Does it make sense to say you have about 30 minutes of the show to watch when you've been watching for 47 minutes? Explain.

_____

(Lesson 5) Regroup 1 ten as 10 ones or 1 hundred as 10 tens. You may use place-value blocks or draw a picture to help.

15. 5 ☐☐
    5 ₆ 4

16. ☐☐ 2
    ₈ 8 2

17. ☐☐ 0
    ₄ 9 0

(Mixed Review) Find each sum.

18. $30 + 60 =$ _____

19. $400 + 300 =$ _____

20. $90 + 20 =$ _____

60 Use with page 160.

Name _____

Practice 4-6

Exploring Subtracting 2-Digit Numbers

1. Find 86 − 48. You may use place-value blocks or draw a picture to help.

   a. Regroup 1 ten for 10 ones in the number 86.

   _____ tens and _____ ones.

   b. Subtract the ones. _____ ones

   c. Subtract the tens. _____ tens

   d. The difference is _____.

Find each difference. You may use place-value blocks or draw a picture to help.

2. 28 − 17 = _____
3. 41 − 6 = _____
4. $97 − $16 = _____
5. 87 − 68 = _____
6. 33 − 25 = _____
7. $55 − $7 = _____
8. 19 − 11 = _____
9. 63 − 6 = _____
10. $77 − $48 = _____
11. 23 − 15 = _____

12. Subtract 23 from 81. _____

13. Find the difference of 63 and 47. _____

14. Find 91 − 52. _____

15. Your class needs to sell 50 tickets to the school show in order to win a prize. So far the class has sold 22 tickets. How many more tickets need to be sold? _____

16. Suppose you had a quarter, 2 dimes, and 7 pennies. If you lost 3 of your pennies, how much money would you have? _____

17. Genevieve has 60 minutes of homework to do. She has done 44 minutes. How many more minutes of homework does she have to do? _____

18. Yuki has read 14 pages of his 51-page book. How many more pages does he have left to read? _____

Use with pages 162–163.

Name _____

Practice 4-7

Subtracting 2-Digit Numbers

Subtract. Check each answer.

1. 76
   −42

2. 63
   −24

3. 34
   − 7

4. $55
   − 13

5. 82
   −54

6. 29
   −18

7. $21
   − 9

8. 70
   −15

9. 32
   − 8

10. 97
   −69

11. 60
   −31

12. 42
   −11

13. 37 − 28 = _____

14. 53 − 15 = _____

15. $24 − $6 = _____

16. 85 − 44 = _____

17. 66 − 39 = _____

18. 41 − 14 = _____

19. Find the difference of 50 and 18. _____

20. Subtract 27 from 42. _____

21. Write two numbers you could subtract from 25 with regrouping.
_____

22. Write two numbers you could subtract from 83 without regrouping.
_____

23. To subtract 22 from 74 do you need to regroup? Explain.
_____

Name _____

Practice 4-10

Subtracting with 2 Regroupings

Subtract. Check each answer.

1. 346
    −167
    ☐☐9

2. 182
    − 95
    ☐7

3. 225
    − 48
    1☐☐

4. 814
    −526
    ☐8☐

5. 751
    −383

6. 427
    −148

7. $83
    − 59

8. 520
    −451

9. 442
    − 86

10. 653
    −275

11. 237
    −179

12. 866
    − 77

13. 413 − 166 = _____

14. 243 − 59 = _____

15. $961 − $585 = _____

16. 92 − 36 = _____

17. 286 − 197 = _____

18. 354 − 188 = _____

19. Find the difference of 365 and 187. _____

20. Subtract 45 from 219. _____

21. Andrea subtracted 736 − 108 and found 628. She then added 736 and 108 to check her answer. Did she check her answer correctly? Explain.

    _____

    _____

22. To find 415 − 136, would you need to regroup hundreds? Explain.

    _____

    _____

Name _____

Practice 4-11

Subtracting Across 0

Subtract. Check each answer.

1. 207
   − 82

2. $403
   − 235

3. 800
   − 38

4. 520
   − 359

5. 309
   − 151

6. 705
   − 467

7. 631
   − 206

8. $104
   − 59

9. 240
   − 198

10. 501
   − 164

11. 408
   − 311

12. 202
   − 28

13. 306 − 147 = _____

14. 500 − 279 = _____

15. 940 − 458 = _____

16. 409 − 45 = _____

17. 604 − 335 = _____

18. 201 − 142 = _____

19. 703 − 497 = _____

20. 506 − 249 = _____

21. What is 703 minus 216? _____

22. Subtract 127 from 400. _____

23. Antonio said, "To solve 506 − 288, I can think of 5 hundreds as 50 tens." How might this help him subtract?

_____

_____

24. Write a number you could subtract from 202 without regrouping.

_____

Name _____

Practice
Chapter 4
Section B

Review and Practice

(Lessons 7 and 9) Subtract. Check each answer.

1. 87
   −38

2. 56
   −27

3. 95
   −54

4. 73
   − 9

5. 371 − 369 = _____
6. 641 − 470 = _____
7. 974 − 58 = _____
8. 356 − 175 = _____
9. 342 − 159 = _____
10. 813 − 645 = _____

(Lessons 10 and 11) Subtract. Check each answer.

11. $870
   − 385

12. 556
    −279

13. 951
    −504

14. 703
    − 99

15. 871 − 119 = _____
16. 601 − 473 = _____
17. 900 − 58 = _____
18. $306 − $177 = _____
19. 801 − 566 = _____
20. 709 − 23 = _____

21. Find the difference of 823 and 179. _____

22. Russia is 62 miles from Alaska. Washington is 500 miles from Alaska. How much farther from Alaska is Washington than Russia? _____

(Mixed Review) Write each time two ways.

23.

24.

25.

_____ _____ _____

_____ _____ _____

Use with page 178. **67**

Name _____

Practice 4-12

Subtracting 4-Digit Numbers: Choose a Calculation Method

Solve. Check each answer.

1. 4,282 − 1,718
2. $6,359 − 3,342
3. 3,200 − 2,000
4. 7,650 − 5,365

5. 2,476 − 1,684
6. 5,699 − 3,940
7. 9,100 − 4,500
8. $4,375 − 3,350

9. 1,671 − 400
10. $6,500 − 999
11. 3,124 − 1,482
12. 8,146 − 7,938

13. 5,442 − 2,200 = _____
14. $6,255 − $1,391 = _____
15. $1,450 − 650 = _____
16. 3,581 − 2,766 = _____
17. 4,733 − 3,627 = _____
18. 7,549 − 4,198 = _____
19. 5,555 − 3,472 = _____
20. 4,356 − 2,987 = _____

21. Subtract 1,234 from 4,321. _____
22. Subtract 6,487 from 7,486. _____
23. Subtract 8,322 from 9,323. _____

24. How could you use mental math to find 1,400 − 500?

_____

25. Leo subtracted 232 from 1,345 on his calculator and found 113. Estimate to check. Is his answer reasonable?

_____

Name _____

Practice 4-13

Analyze Word Problems: Multiple-Step Problems

Solve each problem.

Movie Admission Prices

Before 6 P.M.

Children under 12	$2
Adults	$5

After 6 P.M.

Children under 12	$3
Adults	$8

1. Mr. and Mrs. Riley want to take their 2 children to the movies. Their children are 5 and 9 years old.

   a. How much will it cost for them to see a movie before 6:00 P.M.? _____

   b. How much more will it cost for them to see a movie after 6:00 P.M.? _____

2. Mr. Ramirez told his 9-year old son that he could have $20 to take his friends to the movies. He wants to invite 4 friends from his class and his 14-year-old brother. How much more money does he need to take everyone to see a movie at 7:00 P.M.? _____

3. A scout troop leader is taking 14 scouts to the movies. Three scouts canceled and 5 more decided to go. How many scouts are going to the movies? _____

4. The manager sold 55 adult tickets and 20 children's tickets for an afternoon movie. How many more adult tickets were sold than children's tickets? _____

Name _____

Practice 4-14

Mental Math

Write what number you would add to each in order to subtract mentally. Subtract.

1. 34 − 19 = _____
   I added _____.

2. 63 − 28 = _____
   I added _____.

3. 62 − 36 = _____
   I added _____.

4. 188 − 9 = _____
   I added _____.

5. 154 − 37 = _____
   I added _____.

6. 156 − 39 = _____
   I added _____.

7. 87 − 28 = _____
   I added _____.

8. 71 − 37 = _____
   I added _____.

9. 92 − 45 = _____
   I added _____.

10. 109 − 69 = _____
    I added _____.

11. 168 − 49 = _____
    I added _____.

12. 144 − 67 = _____
    I added _____.

13. What could you add to each number to find 730 − 260? Explain.

    _____

    _____

14. Would you add on to help you find 58 − 20? Explain.

    _____

    _____

Name _____

Practice 4-15

Subtracting Money

Subtract.

1. $5.86
  − 2.55

2. $20.00
  − 7.05

3. $7.00
  − 5.76

4. $6.25
  − 2.98

5. $10.00
  − 5.87

6. $8.75
  − 4.35

7. $8.28
  − 4.99

8. $15.00
  − 3.89

9. $8.98
  − 2.79

10. $17.00
  − 6.72

11. $6.87
  − 1.98

12. $5.24
  − 4.25

13. $6.50 − $2.17 = _____

14. $11.50 − $6.75 = _____

15. $13.85 − $5.98 = _____

16. $20.00 − $8.88 = _____

17. $9.89 − $3.57 = _____

18. $15.00 − $7.99 = _____

19. Rachel bought a puzzle for $4.89. She gave the clerk $10.00. How much change did she receive? _____

20. Diego bought a toy and paid with $5.00. He received $3.29 in change. How much did the toy cost? _____

21. Sophie is buying toothpaste. Superclean costs $4.89 and Sparkles cost $3.24. How much will Sophie save if she buys Sparkles? _____

22. Sophie pays for Sparkles toothpaste with a $5 bill. How much change will she receive? _____

Name _____

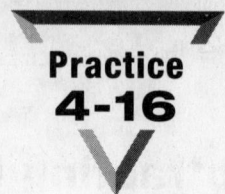

Analyze Strategies: Use Objects

Use objects to help solve each problem.

1. Kendra is going to a hockey game at the arena. She climbs 2 steps at a time to get to the door faster. Her little brother climbs 1 step at a time.

   a. When Kendra has climbed 6 steps, how many steps has her brother taken? _____

   b. When Kendra has climbed 12 steps, how many steps has her brother taken? _____

2. Keith is waiting in line to buy snacks. There are 8 people ahead of him. Two people leave the line without buying anything. Four people buy their snacks and go to their seats. How many people are ahead of him now? _____

3. Doug counts the pennies in his piggy bank. His sister has two pennies for every one penny Doug has. Doug has 9 pennies. How many pennies does his sister have? _____

4. Sheila lives 3 times as far from the school as Julia. If it takes Julia 5 minutes to walk to school, how long will it take Sheila? _____

5. From school, Kathy walks 2 blocks, then 1 block to mail a letter. She walks on 4 more blocks toward home. How many blocks does she walk in all? _____

Use any strategy to help you solve this problem.

6. Shandra rode her bike 1 mile to school. It took her 15 minutes. How long should it take Shandra to ride her bike 3 miles to the bookstore? _____

Name _____

Practice
Chapter 4
Section C

Review and Practice

(Lesson 12) Solve. Check each answer.

1. 5,738
   − 2,667

2. 6,300
   − 4,000

3. 7,856
   − 2,133

4. 5,000
   − 4,025

(Lesson 13) Solve.

5. It cost $3 for a child's ticket and $5 for an adult's ticket at the museum. Peter is going to the museum with his two sisters, Uncle Joe, and his mother. Peter and his 2 sisters can each get child's tickets. How much will it cost? _____

(Lesson 14) Write what number you would add to each in order to subtract mentally. Subtract.

6. 64 − 45 = _____
   Add: _____

7. 372 − 68 = _____
   Add: _____

8. 134 − 29 = _____
   Add: _____

(Lesson 15) Subtract.

9. $4.56
   − 1.38

10. $3.89
    − 2.99

11. $9.00
    − 3.46

12. $15.89
    − 9.69

(Lesson 16) Use objects or any strategy to solve.

13. Tippy woke up at 7:00 A.M. She played for 1 hour. Then she napped. She woke up to play for another hour. Then she slept until Maggie came home from school at 3:00 P.M. How many hours did Tippy sleep? _____

(Mixed Review) Write each time.

14. Elizabeth did her homework at 4:30 P.M. and ate dinner 1 hour and 20 minutes later. What time did she eat? _____

15. Jerome got dressed for school at 7:15 A.M. Eight and a half hours later he returned home. What time was it when Jerome got home? _____

Use with page 194.

Name _____

Practice
Chapters 1–4

Cumulative Review
(Chapter 2 Lesson 13)

1. Brooke starts school at 8:10 A.M. School lets out at 3:25 P.M. How long is Brooke's school day? _____

   A. 8 hours
   B. 7 hours, 35 minutes
   C. 7 hours, 15 minutes
   D. 5 hours, 15 minutes

(Chapter 3 Lesson 14)

2. Clark bought a sandwich for a total of $2.35. He gave the sales person a $5 bill. What is the amount of change he should receive? _____

   A. $3, 6 dimes, and 1 nickel
   B. $2, 6 dimes, and 1 nickel
   C. $2, 5 dimes, and 5 pennies

(Chapter 3 Lesson 15)

3. $2.19
   + 1.97

4. $3.05
   + 1.50

5. $6.89
   + 3.27

6. Find the sum of $8.78 and $3.29. _____

7. What is the sum of $12.15 and $8.29? _____

   A. $10.44   B. $20.14   C. $20.44   D. not here

(Chapter 4 Lessons 7–9)

Find each difference.

8. 56
   − 12

9. 27
   − 9

10. 342
   − 116

11. 2,892
   − 1,451

12. Find the difference of 517 and 230. _____

13. Subtract 338 from 522. _____

74 Use with page 199.

Name _____

Practice 5-1

Exploring Equal Groups
Complete.

1. ○○○○○○○
   ○○○○○○○

   a. _____ + _____ = _____
   b. _____ rows of _____ equals _____.

2. ○○○   ○○○   ○○○

   a. _____ + _____ + _____ = _____
   b. _____ groups of _____ equals _____.

3. ○○○○○
   ○○○○○
   ○○○○○
   ○○○○○

   a. _____ + _____ + _____ + _____ = _____
   b. _____ rows of _____ equals _____.

4. ○○○   ○○○   ○○○
   ○○○   ○○○   ○○○

   a. _____ + _____ + _____ = _____
   b. _____ groups of _____ equals _____.

5. Do these counters show equal groups? Explain.

Use with pages 204–205. **75**

Name _____

Practice
5-2

Writing Multiplication Sentences

Complete each number sentence.

1.

   a. _____ + _____ + _____ = _____
   b. _____ × _____ = _____

2.

   a. _____ + _____ = _____
   b. _____ × _____ = _____

3.

   a. _____ + _____ + _____ + _____ = _____
   b. _____ × _____ = _____

4. Draw a picture that shows 3 × 4. Find the product.

5. Can you multiply to find the total of 9 + 9 + 9? Explain.

   _____

6. Can you multiply to find the total of 3 + 4 + 5? Explain.

   _____

76 Use with pages 206–207.

Name _____

**Practice
5-3**

Exploring Multiplication Stories

1. Is this a multiplication story? Explain.

    Sam makes shirts. He sold 3 shirts one day, and 4 the next day. How many shirts did Sam sell?

    _____

Write a multiplication story for 2–6.
You may use counters to solve.

2. 2×5

    _____

    _____

3. 3×6

    _____

    _____

4. 4×4

    _____

    _____

5. 6×2

    _____

    _____

6. 6×4

    _____

    _____

Solve.

7. There are 6 cars in the parking lot. Each car has 4 tires. How many tires are there?

    _____

Name _____

Practice
Chapter 5
Section A

Review and Practice

Vocabulary Match each with its definition.

_____ 1. product   a. one of the numbers multiplied

_____ 2. factor   b. an arrangement of rows and columns

_____ 3. array   c. the number obtained by multiplying numbers

(Lessons 1 and 2) Complete.

4.
a. ☐ + ☐ + ☐ + ☐ = ☐
b. ☐ groups of ☐ equals ☐.
c. ☐ × ☐ = ☐

5.
a. ☐ + ☐ = ☐
b. ☐ groups of ☐ equals ☐.
c. ☐ × ☐ = ☐

6. Idaho has 2 representatives in the House of Representatives. Minnesota has 4 times as many. How many representatives does Minnesota have?

_____

7. Is the product of 7 × 3 the same as the product of 3 × 7? Explain.

_____

_____

(Lesson 3) Write a multiplication story for each. You may use counters to solve.

8. 4 × 5 = _____

_____

9. 3 × 7 = _____

_____

(Mixed Review) Add or subtract.

10. 23 + 17 = _____   11. 45 − 20 = _____   12. 58 + 26 = _____

78   Use with page 210.

Name _____

Practice 5-4

2 as a Factor

Find each product.

1. $3 \times 2 =$ _____
2. $5 \times 2 =$ _____
3. $2 \times 1 =$ _____
4. $2 \times 10 =$ _____
5. $2 \times 9 =$ _____
6. $8 \times 2 =$ _____
7. $4 \times 2 =$ _____
8. $6 \times 2 =$ _____
9. $2 \times 2 =$ _____
10. $2 \times 7 =$ _____

11. 4
    $\times 2$

12. 2
    $\times 5$

13. 6
    $\times 2$

14. 8
    $\times 2$

15. 9
    $\times 2$

16. 10
    $\times 2$

17. 7
    $\times 2$

18. 2
    $\times 1$

19. 2
    $\times 3$

20. 10
    $\times 2$

21. Find the product of 5 and 2. _____
22. Find the product of 2 and 8. _____
23. Find the product of 10 and 2. _____
24. Find the product of 6 and 2. _____
25. Find the product of 7 and 2. _____
26. Find the product of 3 and 2. _____

27. Is the product of 5 and 2 the same as the sum of 5 and 2? Explain.

_____

28. Draw a picture to show that 7×2 is the same as 2×7.

Use with pages 212–213.

Name _____

Practice 5-5

5 as a Factor

Find each product.

1. $2 \times 5 =$ _____
2. $5 \times 5 =$ _____
3. $5 \times 1 =$ _____
4. $5 \times 8 =$ _____
5. $2 \times 9 =$ _____
6. $3 \times 5 =$ _____
7. $5 \times 4 =$ _____
8. $5 \times 6 =$ _____
9. $5 \times 7 =$ _____
10. $2 \times 8 =$ _____

11. 4
    $\times 5$

12. 5
    $\times 5$

13. 6
    $\times 2$

14. 5
    $\times 8$

15. 9
    $\times 5$

16. 8
    $\times 2$

17. 7
    $\times 2$

18. 2
    $\times 1$

19. 2
    $\times 3$

20. 8
    $\times 5$

21. 5
    $\times 2$

22. 7
    $\times 5$

23. 8
    $\times 5$

24. 6
    $\times 5$

25. 3
    $\times 5$

26. Find the product of 5 and 7. _____

27. Multiply 8 by 5. _____

28. If you know the product of 8 and 5, how can you use it to find 9×5?

_____

29. Is 7×5 greater or less than 8×5? Explain.

_____

Name _____

Practice 5-6

Exploring Patterns on a Hundred Chart: 2s and 5s

Finish these sentences.

1. a. Multiples of 2 always end in _____.

   b. Write some multiplication sentences to show the pattern:
   _____

2. a. Multiples of 5 always end in _____.

   b. Write some multiplication sentences to show the pattern:
   _____

Find each product.

3. $8 \times 2 =$ _____ 4. $8 \times 5 =$ _____ 5. $2 \times 2 =$ _____

6. $7 \times 5 =$ _____ 7. $2 \times 7 =$ _____ 8. $5 \times 4 =$ _____

9. $6 \times 5 =$ _____ 10. $2 \times 9 =$ _____ 11. $2 \times 10 =$ _____

12. 4   13. 6   14. 9   15. 2
    × 2   × 2   × 5   × 1

16. 5   17. 3   18. 5   19. 2
    × 6   × 2   × 1   × 5

20. Find the product of 5 and 3. _____

21. Multiply 6 by 2. _____

22. What numbers are shaded twice when you shade multiples of 2s and multiples of 5s on a hundred chart?
    _____

Use with pages 216–217. **81**

Name _____

Practice 5-7

Exploring 0 and 1 as Factors

Finish these sentences.

1. a. The product of any number and 1 is _____.

   b. Write a multiplication sentence to show this.

   _____

2. a. The product of any number and 0 is _____.

   b. Write a multiplication sentence to show this.

   _____

Find each product.

3. $8 \times 0 =$ _____ 4. $8 \times 1 =$ _____ 5. $0 \times 2 =$ _____

6. $1 \times 5 =$ _____ 7. $2 \times 1 =$ _____ 8. $5 \times 4 =$ _____

9. $5 \times 5 =$ _____ 10. $2 \times 9 =$ _____

11. 4
    × 2

12. 6
    × 1

13. 9
    × 0

14. 2
    × 1

15. 1
    × 6

16. 3
    × 2

17. 5
    × 1

18. 1
    × 5

19. 0
    × 3

20. 1
    × 3

21. 0
    × 1

22. 0
    × 0

23. Find the product of 1 and 1. _____

24. Multiply 0 by 1. _____

Complete. Write × or +.

25. 8 _____ 1 = 9   26. 9 _____ 1 = 9   27. 0 _____ 5 = 5

28. 2 _____ 10 = 20 29. 2 _____ 0 = 0   30. 5 _____ 5 = 10

82   Use with pages 218–219.

Name _____

Practice 5-8

9 as a Factor
Find each product.

1. $9 \times 8 =$ _____
2. $4 \times 9 =$ _____
3. $9 \times 7 =$ _____
4. $9 \times 6 =$ _____
5. $5 \times 9 =$ _____
6. $0 \times 5 =$ _____
7. $9 \times 3 =$ _____
8. $3 \times 5 =$ _____
9. $2 \times 6 =$ _____

10.   9
  × 9
  ―――

11.   8
  × 5
  ―――

12.   2
  × 7
  ―――

13.   9
  × 8
  ―――

14.   5
  × 4
  ―――

15.   1
  × 9
  ―――

16.   7
  × 5
  ―――

17.   9
  × 0
  ―――

18. Find the product of 8 and 9. _____

19. Multiply 9 by 2. _____

20. If you forget the product of 9 and 9, what can you do to figure it out?

_____

_____

21. Is 6×9 the same as 9×7? Explain.

_____

22. Is 5×9 the same as 6×9? Explain.

_____

23. Write a number sentence that shows the same product as the product of 9 and 2.

_____

Name _____

Practice 5-9

Analyze Word Problems: Too Much or Too Little Information

Decide if the problem has too much or too little information. Then solve. If there is not enough information, tell what information is needed.

1. It takes about 3 months to grow tomatoes. The vines should be planted about 2 feet apart and get a lot of sun. If Taylor wants to plant 6 tomato vines in a row, how long should the row be?

   Too much or too little information? _____

   How do you solve it? _____

   _____

2. Each tomato vine can grow about 25 tomatoes. Taylor wants to make 3 gallons of spaghetti sauce with his tomatoes. Will 6 vines be enough?

   Too much or too little information? _____

   How do you solve it? _____

   _____

3. Kathryn is going to knit a sweater that is red and yellow. She needs 6 skeins of red yarn. If each skein is 100 meters long, how many meters of yarn will she need all together?

   Too much or too little information? _____

   How do you solve it? _____

   _____

4. A piano keyboard has a total of 88 black and white keys. 36 of these are black. It takes 13 keys to play an octave. How many keys are white?

   Too much or too little information? _____

   How do you solve it? _____

   _____

Use with pages 224–225.

Name _____

Practice 5-10

Analyze Strategies: Draw a Picture

Draw a picture to help you solve.

1. How many bricks will Julia need to build a garden wall 9 bricks long and 8 bricks high? _____

2. Julia wants to build another garden wall, 10 bricks long and 3 bricks high. Can she build it with red and white bricks, so that no two bricks of the same color are next to each other? _____

Draw a picture or use any strategy to solve the problems.

3. Ray is setting the table for a birthday dinner. He needs to set 12 places at a round table. He has 3 different kinds of plates: white plates; blue plates; and gold plates. How can he set the table so that no two of the same kind of plates are next to each other?

_____

4. Ray has 13 forks, 15 spoons, and 11 dinner knives. If 12 people are coming to dinner does he have enough silverware so that each person can have a fork, spoon and dinner knife?

_____

Use with pages 226–227. **85**

Name _____

Practice
Chapter 5
Section B

Review and Practice

(Lessons 4–8) Find each product.

1. 3
   × 2

2. 5
   × 8

3. 8
   × 2

4. 4
   × 9

5. 9
   × 0

6. 5
   × 7

7. 9
   × 2

8. 1
   × 5

9. 5
   × 2

10. 7
    × 2

11. 3 × 5 = _____

12. 1 × 2 = _____

13. 6 × 2 = _____

14. 9 × 5 = _____

15. 5 × 4 = _____

16. 2 × 2 = _____

17. List 5 multiples of 3. _____

(Lessons 9 and 10) Solve.

18. Harold gave each of his nine friends three stickers. Four of the stickers were red. How many stickers did he give away? _____

19. Pamela has 2 boxes of crayons. Each box has 48 crayons in it. 8 of the crayons are sharpened. How many crayons does she have? _____

20. Michele and 2 friends each live on a different floor of a three-story apartment building. Shaun lives above Barb and below Michele. Who lives on the first floor? _____

(Mixed Review) Continue each pattern.

21. 7, 14, 21, 28, _____, _____, _____

22. 18, 27, 36, 45, _____, _____, _____

23. 10, 12, 14, 16, _____, _____, _____

Use with page 230.

Name _____

Practice
Chapters 1–5

Cumulative Review

(Chapter 3, Lesson 13) Solve.

1. Sue Ann has $3.50 in quarters and $1.15 in nickels. How many quarters does she have? How many nickels? How much money does she have in all?

   _____

(Chapter 2, Lesson 7) Write each set of numbers in order from greatest to least.

2. 470, 704, 740, 407 _____

3. 400,100; 410,000; 401,700; 407,100

   _____

(Chapter 3, Lesson 7) Find each sum.

4. 326   5. 412   6. 319   7. 828
   +719   +811   +324   +124

(Chapter 4, Lesson 10) Find each difference.

8. 314   9. 427   10. 516   11. 644
   −126   −189   −427   −356

12. 818 − 529 = _____   13. 745 − 266 = _____

(Chapter 5, Lessons 4 and 5) Find each product.

14. 3   15. 4   16. 5   17. 2   18. 6
    ×5   ×2   ×8   ×9   ×5

19. 7 × 5 = _____   20. 2 × 6 = _____   21. 7 × 2 = _____

Use with page 235. **87**

Name _____

Practice 6-1

3 as a Factor: Using Known Facts

Find each product.

1. 8 × 3
2. 3 × 1
3. 6 × 3
4. 7 × 3
5. 3 × 2

6. 3 × 3
7. 4 × 3
8. 9 × 3
9. 3 × 8
10. 5 × 3

11. 3 × 2 _____
12. 6 × 3 _____
13. 3 × 5 _____
14. 3 × 9 _____

15. 8 × 3 _____
16. 1 × 3 _____
17. 7 × 3 _____
18. 4 × 3 _____

19. What is the product of 9 and 3? _____

20. What is the product of 6 and 3? _____

21. Multiply 5 by 3. _____

22. Multiply 3 by 4. _____

23. If you know the product of 2 × 6, how can you find the product of 3 × 6? What is it?

_____

24. Tim says, "To find 3 × 8, I can find 2 × 8 and add one more group of 3." What's wrong? Explain.

_____

Use with pages 240–241.

Name _____

Practice
6-2

4 as a Factor: Doubling

Find each product.

1. 4
   × 5

2. 6
   × 4

3. 9
   × 4

4. 4
   × 3

5. 1
   × 4

6. 8
   × 2

7. 4
   × 8

8. 4
   × 4

9. 2
   × 4

10. 4
    × 7

11. 5 × 4 _____

12. 4 × 9 _____

13. 4 × 2 _____

14. 4 × 4 _____

15. 1 × 4 _____

16. 6 × 4 _____

17. 3 × 4 _____

18. 7 × 4 _____

19. Multiply 8 by 4.
    _____

20. Multiply 4 by 7.
    _____

21. What is the product of 4 and 9? _____

22. What is the product of 4 and 5? _____

23. Draw arrays to show that 4 × 5 is the same as 5 × 4.

24. Could you use doubling to multiply 7 × 3? Explain.

    _____

    _____

Use with pages 242–243.

Name _____

Practice 6-3

6 as a Factor: Using Known Facts
Find each product.

1. 0
   $\times 6$

2. 3
   $\times 6$

3. 6
   $\times 5$

4. 9
   $\times 6$

5. 6
   $\times 6$

6. 6
   $\times 2$

7. 1
   $\times 6$

8. 7
   $\times 6$

9. 6
   $\times 4$

10. 6
    $\times 8$

11. 6×4
    _____

12. 2×6
    _____

13. 9×6
    _____

14. 6×0
    _____

15. 5×6
    _____

16. 6×8
    _____

17. 6×6
    _____

18. 3×6
    _____

19. Find the product of 6 and 7.
    _____

20. What is 9 multiplied by 6?
    _____

21. Find the product of 6 and 6.
    _____

22. What is 3 multiplied by 6?
    _____

23. Which is greater, 6×9 or 9×5? How can you tell without multiplying?

    _____
    _____

24. Can you think of a way to use doubling to multiply 6×7? Explain.

    _____
    _____

90 Use with pages 244–245.

Name _____

Practice 6-4

7 and 8 as Factors
Find each product.

1. 7
   × 8

2. 8
   × 9

3. 9
   × 7

4. 6
   × 8

5. 4
   × 8

6. 3
   × 7

7. 7
   × 7

8. 5
   × 8

9. 8
   × 8

10. 4
   × 7

11. 6 × 7 _____

12. 8 × 7 _____

13. 0 × 7 _____

14. 8 × 2 _____

15. 8 × 0 _____

16. 7 × 7 _____

17. 2 × 7 _____

18. 9 × 7 _____

19. Find the product of 8 and 9. _____

20. Find the product of 7 and 6. _____

21. Find the product of 7 and 8. _____

22. Find the product of 8 and 5. _____

23. How could you find the product of 7 × 8 if you know the product of 5 × 8?

_____

24. How can you tell that 7 × 6 is greater than 6 × 5 without multiplying?

_____

Use with pages 246–247. **91**

Name _____

Practice 6-5

Decision Making

Annie is a party planner. She must plan the menu for 3 dinners; one for 4 people, one for 7 people, and one for 8 people. She needs to make a table to find out how many of each item will be needed for each dinner.

Complete the table.

Number per Serving	4-Person Dinner	7-Person Dinner	8-Person Dinner
6 snack crackers	24	42	48
4 potatoes			
2 chicken pieces			
7 baby carrots			
3 broccoli spears			
8 parsley sprigs			
7 strawberries			
1 mint			

1. How many baby carrots will Annie need for the 8-person dinner? _____

2. How many chicken pieces will she need for the 7-person dinner? _____

3. Annie decides she wants to serve cream with the strawberries. She needs 3 spoonfuls for each person. How many spoonfuls does she need for:

   a. the 4-person dinner? _____

   b. the 7-person dinner? _____

   c. the 8-person dinner? _____

4. One of the people at the 7-person dinner can't go. How many chicken pieces will Annie need for that dinner now? _____

5. An extra person will be going to the 4-person dinner. How many strawberries will Annie need for that dinner now? _____

Name _____

Practice 6-7

Exploring Patterns on a Fact Table

Look for patterns in multiples of greater numbers.

1. What is the pattern for multiples of 10?

   _____

2. What is the pattern for multiples of 11?

   _____

3. What is the pattern for multiples of 12?

   _____

Find each product.

4. 9×9

5. 7×8

6. 6×12

7. 10×11

8. 8×5

9. 7×9

10. 12×7

11. 11×11

12. 12×6

13. 7×10

14. 12×9

15. 11×3

Continue each pattern.

16. 33, 44, 55, _____, _____, _____

17. 72, 60, 48, _____, _____, _____

18. 0, 20, 40, _____, _____, _____

19. 132, 110, 88, _____, _____, _____

20. 48, 60, 72, _____, _____, _____

Practice 6-8

Multiplying with 3 Factors

Find each product.

1. $(4 \times 3) \times 2$
2. $1 \times (6 \times 8)$
3. $9 \times 1 \times 7$

4. $5 \times (3 \times 3)$
5. $2 \times 1 \times 5$
6. $(0 \times 1) \times 8$

7. $2 \times 0 \times 9$
8. $3 \times (2 \times 5)$
9. $6 \times (6 \times 1)$

10. $(3 \times 2) \times 7$
11. $1 \times 7 \times 4$
12. $(2 \times 0) \times 8$

13. $(3 \times 6) \times 0$
14. $(2 \times 12) \times 1$
15. $6 \times 3 \times 3$

16. Find the product of 1, 7, and 6. _____
17. Find the product of 9, 4, and 0. _____

18. Does 6×4 have the same product as $3 \times 4 \times 2$? Explain.

19. If you know the product of $5 \times 2 \times 3$, do you also know the product of $3 \times 2 \times 5$? Explain.

Name _____

Practice 6-9

Compare Strategies: Look for a Pattern and Draw a Picture

Use any strategy to solve each problem.

1. Suppose you are planning a picnic for 34 people. You must buy paper plates in packages of 8. How many packages of paper plates will you need? _____

2. One package of rolls has enough rolls for 8 burgers. How many packages of rolls do you need for 25 burgers? _____

3. Your softball team has a party. Everyone uses 4 napkins. If there are 13 people at the party, how many napkins were used? _____

4. One loaf of bread makes 10 sandwiches. How many loaves do you need to make 54 sandwiches?
_____

5. You are making pizza for a party. Each pizza has 8 slices.
    a. If 93 people will be at the party, how many pizzas should you make so that each person gets one slice?
    _____
    b. How many slices will be left over? _____

6. Each jug of juice serves 12 people. How many jugs will you need for 60 people? _____

Name _____

Practice
Chapter 6
Section B

Review and Practice

(Lesson 6) Write true or false. You may use a hundred chart to help.

1. 42 is a multiple of 6. _____
2. 41 is a multiple of 3. _____
3. 83 is a multiple of 3 and 6. _____
4. All multiples of 6 are also multiples of 3. _____

(Lesson 7) Continue each pattern.

5. 18, 27, 36, _____, _____, _____
6. 36, 48, 60, _____, _____, _____
7. How can you tell without multiplying that 6 × 10 does not equal 66?

_____

(Lesson 8) Find each product.

8. $5 \times 2 \times 8 =$ _____
9. $1 \times 9 \times 4 =$ _____
10. $0 \times 7 \times 1 =$ _____
11. $3 \times 2 \times 7 =$ _____
12. $2 \times (2 \times 3) =$ _____
13. $(6 \times 1) \times 5 =$ _____

(Lesson 9) Solve. Use any strategy.

14. You want to send cards to 37 people. The cards you want to send come in packages of 6. How many packages will you need? _____

15. While on vacation Marsha sent 35 postcards. She sent 7 postcards from each city she visited. How many cities did she visit? _____

(Mixed Review) Continue each pattern.

16. 48, 45, 42, _____, _____, _____
17. 6, 10, 14, 18, _____, _____, _____
18. 12, 24, 36, _____, _____, _____

Use with page 266.

Name _____

Practice
Chapters 1–6

Cumulative Review

(Chapter 3 Lesson 9) Find each sum.

1. 35
    66
   +88

2. 84
    28
   +53

3. 679
     44
   +345

4. 71
    93
   +309

5. Patricia earned 96, 95, and 87 on three math tests. She needs a total of 279 points to get an A average. Does she have enough points for an A? Explain.

_____

(Chapter 4 Lesson 11) Find each difference.

6. 800
   − 58

7. 907
   −628

8. 600
   −299

9. 200
   −184

(Chapter 5 Lesson 4) Find each product.

10. 8
   × 2

11. 2
   × 4

12. 2
   × 5

13. 7
   × 2

14. 9
   × 2

(Chapter 6 Lessons 1–3) Find each product.

15. 3
   × 2

16. 4
   × 3

17. 4
   × 5

18. 7
   × 4

19. 9
   × 6

20. 8
   × 3

21. 6
   × 4

22. 3
   × 6

23. 7
   × 6

24. 9
   × 3

Use with page 271.   **99**

Name _____

Practice
7-1

Exploring Division as Sharing

Mrs. Robbins and Mrs. Siani are making up flower baskets for a wedding celebration. They have to do 6 baskets in all. They decide to share the work equally. How many baskets will each prepare?

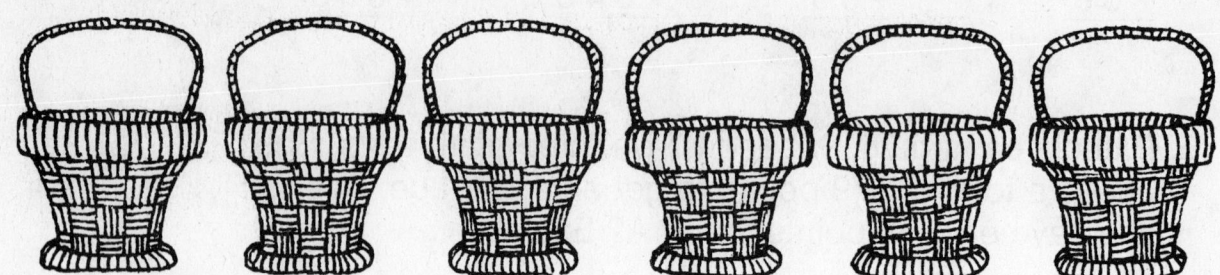

1. Draw a line to divide the baskets into 2 equal groups.

2. 6 flower baskets ÷ 2 women = _____ baskets each.

Complete. You may use counters or draw pictures to help.

3. 8 ÷ 2 = _____

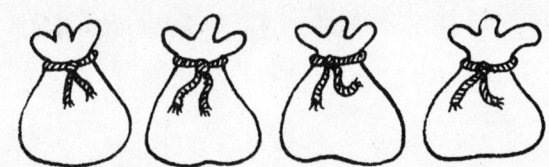

4. 16 ÷ 4 = _____

Solve. You may use counters or draw pictures to help.

5. Misha and Angie have volunteered to call 10 people to raise money for their Girl Scout troop. If they divide the calls equally, how many calls will each girl make?

_____

6. You are helping the school yearbook editor. There are 24 pictures that will go on 3 pages in the yearbook. How many photos will you put on each page if you divide them evenly?

_____

Name _____

Practice 7-2

Exploring Division as Repeated Subtraction

Maria is pouring glasses of iced tea. She has 18 ice cubes. If she wants to put 6 ice cubes in each glass, how many glasses can she fill?

1. Draw lines to show 6 ice cubes per glass.

2. 18 ice cubes ÷ 6 per glass = _____ glasses.

Complete. You may use counters or complete the pictures to help.

3. 10 letters

2 in each mailbox

10 ÷ 2 = _____

4. 12 flowers

3 in each pot

12 ÷ 3 = _____

5. Brenda puts 3 cookies on each plate. Can she make 5 plates with 15 cookies? Draw a picture and explain.

_____

_____

Use with pages 278–279. **101**

Name _____

Practice 7-3

Exploring Division Stories

1. Three friends share a 6-pack of juice equally. How many cans of juice does each one drink?

   6 ÷ 3 = _____ cans

2. Telia made 15 snowflake ornaments. If she gives 3 to each of her friends, how many friends will get ornaments?

   15 ÷ 3 = _____ friends

Write a division story for each. You may use counters to solve.

3. 8 ÷ 4 = _____

   _____
   _____

4. 21 ÷ 7 = _____

   _____
   _____

Complete each number sentence. You may use counters to solve.

5. 16 ÷ _____ = 2   6. 24 ÷ _____ = 8   7. 36 ÷ _____ = 4

Solve. You may use counters or draw pictures to help.

8. Dana has 10 free show tickets. He can give away 2 to each person in his family. How many people are in his family?

   _____

9. Beth's book has 28 pages. She reads 4 pages each day. How long will it take her to finish the book? _____

10. Michael used 12 slices of cheese to make 4 equal-sized sandwiches. How many slices of cheese did he put in each sandwich? _____

Name _____

Practice
Chapter 7
Section A

Review and Practice

(Lessons 1 and 2) Use the pictures to help you complete each number sentence.

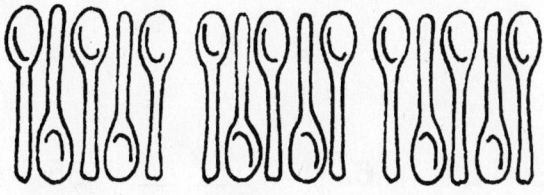 

1. 15 ÷ 3 = _____   **2.** 10 ÷ 2 = _____

3. 14 ÷ 7 = _____   **4.** 8 ÷ 4 = _____

5. Natalie and her two brothers have $12 to spend on lunch. One Kid's Meal costs $3. Do they have enough money? Explain how you know.

_____

(Lesson 3) Write a division story for each. You may use counters to solve.

6. 20 ÷ 4 = _____

_____

7. 18 ÷ 9 = _____

_____

(Mixed Review) Complete each number sentence.

8. _____ + 8 = 13   **9.** _____ − 9 = 5   **10.** 6 + _____ = 11

Use with page 282. **103**

Name _____

Practice 7-4

Connecting Multiplication and Division

Complete. You may use counters to help.

1. $7 \times$ _____ $= 28$
   $28 \div 7 =$ _____

2. $6 \times$ _____ $= 42$
   $42 \div 6 =$ _____

3. $2 \times$ _____ $= 12$
   $12 \div 2 =$ _____

4. $2 \times$ _____ $= 18$
   $18 \div 2 =$ _____

5. $3 \times$ _____ $= 21$
   $21 \div 3 =$ _____

6. $7 \times$ _____ $= 35$
   $35 \div 7 =$ _____

7. $2 \times$ _____ $= 6$
   $6 \div 2 =$ _____

8. $5 \times$ _____ $= 25$
   $25 \div 5 =$ _____

9. $6 \times$ _____ $= 12$
   $12 \div 6 =$ _____

10. $4 \times$ _____ $= 32$
    $32 \div 4 =$ _____

11. $3 \times$ _____ $= 30$
    $30 \div 3 =$ _____

12. $8 \times$ _____ $= 24$
    $24 \div 8 =$ _____

13. What multiplication fact could you use to solve $24 \div 3$?
    _____

14. What are the number sentences in the fact family with $32 \div 4 = 8$?
    _____

15. What multiplication fact could you use to solve $20 \div 2$?
    _____

16. What are the number sentences in the fact family with $24 \div 4 = 6$?
    _____

Name _____

Practice 7-7

Dividing by 3 and 4
Find each quotient.

1. $3\overline{)15}$
2. $4\overline{)8}$
3. $4\overline{)12}$

4. $5\overline{)30}$
5. $3\overline{)6}$
6. $3\overline{)21}$

7. $4\overline{)28}$
8. $4\overline{)20}$
9. $3\overline{)12}$

10. $2\overline{)10}$
11. $3\overline{)18}$
12. $4\overline{)32}$

13. $27 \div 3 =$ _____
14. $9 \div 3 =$ _____
15. $24 \div 4 =$ _____
16. $24 \div 3 =$ _____
17. $25 \div 5 =$ _____
18. $16 \div 4 =$ _____
19. $14 \div 2 =$ _____
20. $36 \div 4 =$ _____

21. Divide 18 by 3. _____

22. Divide 20 by 4. _____

23. How many 4s are in 28? _____

24. How many 3s are in 15? _____

25. How many 4s are in 40? _____

26. How many 3s are in 30? _____

27. How could you take away equal groups to find $4\overline{)12}$?

_____

Name _____

Practice 7-8

Exploring Dividing with 0 and 1

Find each quotient. Complete the division rule.

1. a. $3 \div 1 =$ _____

   b. Rule: Any number divided by 1 equals _____.

2. a. $5 \div 5 =$ _____

   b. Rule: Any number (except 0) divided by itself equals _____.

3. a. $0 \div 2 =$ _____

   b. Rule: Zero divided by any number (except 0) equals _____.

4. Can you divide by 0? _____

Find each quotient. Write the division rule that explains the answer.

5. $4 \div 4 =$ _____

   Rule: _____

6. $0 \div 7 =$ _____

   Rule: _____

7. $8 \div 1 =$ _____

   Rule: _____

Write >, <, or =.

8. $6 \div 6 \bigcirc 3 \div 3$

9. $12 \div 4 \bigcirc 12 \div 3$

10. $25 \div 5 \bigcirc 0 \div 5$

11. $4 \div 1 \bigcirc 6 \div 1$

12. $6 \div 2 \bigcirc 3 \div 1$

13. $0 \div 4 \bigcirc 4 \div 2$

14. $8 \div 4 \bigcirc 4 \div 2$

15. $10 \div 5 \bigcirc 5 \div 5$

Name _____

Practice 7-9

Analyze Word Problems: Choose an Operation

Which number sentence would you use to solve the problem? Explain.

1. Suppose Blair worked 6 hours a week for 3 weeks. How many hours did she work?

   A. $6 + 3 = 9$ **B.** $6 \times 3 = 18$ **C.** $6 - 3 = 3$ **D.** $18 + 6 = 24$

   _____

2. Marcie sold $8 worth of fruit tarts at a bake sale. Each tart cost $2. How many tarts did she sell?

   A. $8 - 2 = 6$ **B.** $8 \div 2 = 4$ **C.** $8 \times 2 = 16$ **D.** $8 + 2 = 10$

   _____

3. Arthur had 6 tickets to a concert. He gave 2 of them to Joe. How many tickets did he have left?

   A. $6 - 2 = 4$ **B.** $6 + 2 = 8$ **C.** $6 \times 2 = 12$ **D.** $6 \div 2 = 3$

   _____

Write which operation you would use. Then solve.

4. Zachary bought 4 bananas and 3 oranges. How many pieces of fruit did he buy?

   _____

5. Lars bought a 2-pound bag of dog food for $2.25 and a 1-pound bag of cat food for $1.54. How much money did he spend?

   _____

6. Isabella earns $4 per hour working at the pet store. If she works for 7 hours, how much money will she earn?

   _____

7. Nick had 16 marbles. He gave an equal number to each of 4 friends. How many marbles did each friend get?

   _____

Name _____

Practice
Chapter 7
Section B

Review and Practice

Vocabulary Write true or false for each statement.

1. In the problem 18 ÷ 2 = 9, the divisor is 9. _____
2. Fact families are groups of related facts using the same set of digits. _____
3. The dividend in the problem 24 ÷ 3 = 8 is 24. _____
4. The quotient in the problem 12 ÷ 4 = 3 is 12. _____

(Lessons 5–8) Find each quotient.

5. 2 ÷ 2 = _____
6. 16 ÷ 4 = _____
7. 20 ÷ 5 = _____
8. 8 ÷ 2 = _____
9. 12 ÷ 3 = _____
10. 40 ÷ 5 = _____
11. 20 ÷ 4 = _____
12. 18 ÷ 3 = _____
13. 14 ÷ 2 = _____
14. 45 ÷ 5 = _____
15. 54 ÷ 1 = _____
16. 0 ÷ 2 = _____
17. 27 ÷ 3 = _____
18. 36 ÷ 4 = _____
19. 0 ÷ 4 = _____
20. 16 ÷ 2 = _____

21. 2)$\overline{18}$
22. 5)$\overline{30}$
23. 3)$\overline{21}$
24. 4)$\overline{8}$

(Lesson 9) Write which operation you would use. Then solve.

25. Selma wants to build bird houses to give as gifts. It takes 4 boards to make one house. Selma has 24 boards. How many bird houses can she make?

   _____

26. Nu has to write 3 reports. Each report must be 2 pages. How many pages must he write?

   _____

(Mixed Review) Find each missing factor.

27. 1 × _____ × 8 = 0
28. 3 × _____ × 2 = 24
29. _____ × 5 × 2 = 20
30. 4 × 1 × _____ = 20

110 Use with page 298.

Name _____

Practice 7-10

Dividing by 6 and 7
Find each quotient.

1. 6)18   2. 7)14   3. 6)24

4. 7)28   5. 6)6   6. 1)7

7. 6)54   8. 7)49   9. 7)42

10. 3)18   11. 6)12   12. 6)36

13. 42 ÷ 6 = _____   14. 7 ÷ 7 = _____   15. 56 ÷ 7 = _____
16. 12 ÷ 6 = _____   17. 63 ÷ 7 = _____   18. 21 ÷ 3 = _____
19. 0 ÷ 6 = _____   20. 30 ÷ 5 = _____   21. 35 ÷ 7 = _____
22. 48 ÷ 6 = _____   23. 24 ÷ 4 = _____   24. 21 ÷ 7 = _____

25. Divide 36 by 6. _____   26. Divide 30 by 6. _____
27. Divide 28 by 4. _____   28. Divide 0 by 7. _____

29. What multiplication fact can help you find 42 ÷ 7?

_____

30. What multiplication fact can help you find 24 ÷ 6 ?

_____

31. Is the quotient of 48 ÷ 6 greater than or less than the quotient of 42 ÷ 7? Explain.

_____

32. Is the quotient of 63 ÷ 7 greater than or less than the quotient of 54 ÷ 6? Explain.

_____

Use with pages 300–301.

Name _____

Practice 7-11

Dividing by 8 and 9
Find each quotient.

1. 8)16   2. 9)36   3. 8)40

4. 9)36   5. 7)21   6. 8)8

7. 9)45   8. 8)72   9. 9)0

10. 4)36   11. 9)63   12. 8)56

13. 81 ÷ 9 = _____   14. 32 ÷ 8 = _____
15. 27 ÷ 9 = _____   16. 9 ÷ 9 = _____
17. 64 ÷ 8 = _____   18. 54 ÷ 9 = _____
19. 72 ÷ 9 = _____   20. 24 ÷ 8 = _____

21. Divide 56 by 8. _____   22. Divide 18 by 9. _____
23. Divide 45 by 9. _____   24. Divide 56 by 7. _____

25. What multiplication fact can help you find 63 ÷ 9?

_____

26. What multiplication fact can help you find 48 ÷ 8?

_____

27. How does knowing 4 × 9 = 36 help you solve 36 ÷ 9?

_____

28. Which is greater, 48 ÷ 6 or 48 ÷ 8? Explain.

_____

29. Which is greater, 81 ÷ 9 or 36 ÷ 4?

_____

Name _____

Practice 7-12

Exploring Even and Odd Numbers

1. Even numbers have 0, _____, 4, _____, or _____ in the ones place.

2. Odd numbers have 1, _____, _____, 7, or _____ in the ones place.

Write odd or even for each. You may use color cubes to help.

3.  _____

4. 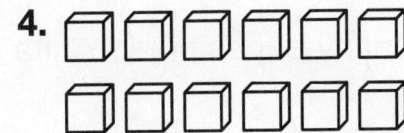 _____

5. 6 _____   6. 19 _____   7. 9 _____   8. 24 _____

9. 18 _____   10. 17 _____   11. 11 _____   12. 23 _____

13. Start with 14 and name the next 5 even numbers. Explain how you know which numbers are even.

_____

_____

14. Add the pairs of odd numbers.
    Do you get even or odd sums? _____

    a. 7 + 5 _____   b. 3 + 9 _____   c. 11 + 7 _____

    d. Can you think of any two odd numbers where the sum of the numbers will be odd? _____

15. Add the pairs of even and odd numbers.
    Do you get even or odd sums? _____

    a. 5 + 16 _____   b. 8 + 7 _____   c. 14 + 5 _____

    d. Can you think of any two numbers, one even and the other odd, in which the sum is an even number? _____

16. Tenisha has two pages in her photo album to fill. She puts 7 photos on each page. Did she have an even or odd number of photos?

    Explain. _____

Name _____

Practice 7-13

Compare Strategies: Use Objects and Make an Organized List

Use any strategy to solve.

1. Anita received 12 new stickers and a new sticker album on her birthday. She wants to put an equal number of stickers on each page that she uses.

   a. How many pages could Anita use in her sticker album?

   _____

   b. How many stickers could be on each page?

   _____

   c. List all the ways Anita could put the stickers in her sticker album.

   _____

   _____

2. Paul has a collection of action figures. He wants to arrange the figures in equal rows. If Paul has 30 action figures, what are all the ways to arrange the figures?

   _____

   _____

3. Juan has 2 pairs of sneakers, one black pair and one white pair. He has 3 baseball caps, one red, one blue and the other orange. What are all the combinations of shoes and caps he could wear?

   _____

   _____

   _____

4. Rosalind must read an 18-page book. She wants to read an equal number of pages every day. List all the possible ways she could divide her reading.

   _____

   _____

114 Use with pages 308–309.

Exploring Algebra: Balancing Scales

Find all the ways to balance each scale. Make a table to record each way. You may use color cubes to help.

1. a. Box A has 8 cubes inside. How many cubes can be in boxes B and C?

Fill in the missing numbers in the table.

A	8	8	8	8	8	8	8	8	8
B	8	7							0
C	0		2	3					

b. 2 cubes have been removed from box A. How many cubes are now in the boxes? Fill in the missing numbers in the table.

A							
B		5			2		0
C	0			3			

2. Box B has 7 cubes inside. Box C has 5 cubes inside. How many cubes are in each box A?

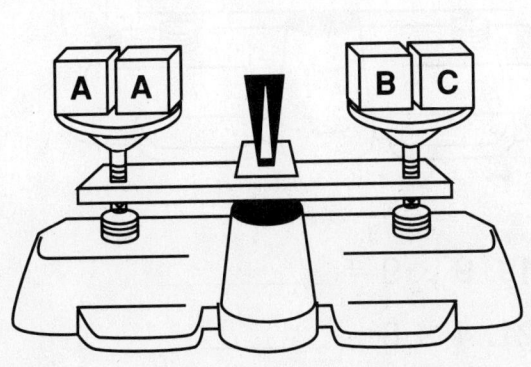

3. Box A has 15 cubes inside. How many cubes are in each box B?

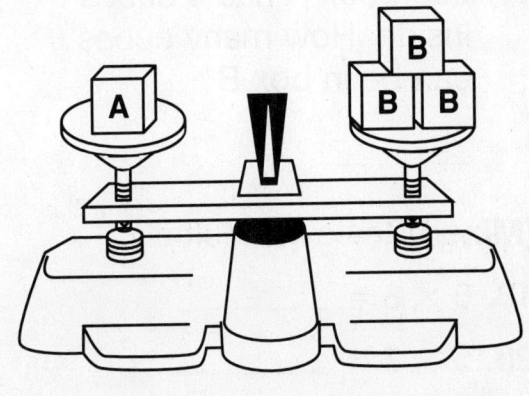

Name _____

Practice
Chapter 7
Section C

Review and Practice

Vocabulary Match the set of numbers with the word describing it.

1. even _____
2. odd _____

a. 26, 32, 24, 48
b. 31, 47, 19, 21

(Lessons 10 and 11) Find each quotient.

3. 12 ÷ 6 = _____
4. 16 ÷ 8 = _____
5. 21 ÷ 7 = _____
6. 28 ÷ 7 = _____
7. 18 ÷ 9 = _____
8. 45 ÷ 9 = _____
9. 24 ÷ 8 = _____
10. 18 ÷ 6 = _____
11. Divide 49 by 7. _____
12. Divide 56 by 8. _____

(Lesson 12) Write odd or even. You may use color cubes to help.

13. 17 _____
14. 36 _____
15. 15 _____

(Lesson 13) Use any strategy to solve.

16. Hunter wants to take a picture of his class. There are 24 students in his class. He wants them to stand in equal rows. What are all the ways he could arrange them?

_____

_____

(Lesson 14) Solve. You may use color cubes to help.

17. Each box A has 4 cubes inside. How many cubes can be in box B?

_____

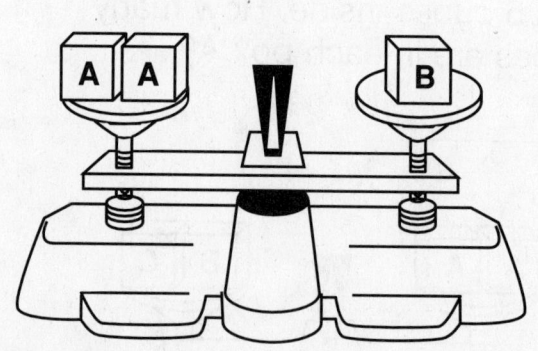

(Mixed Review) Multiply.

18. 6 × 8 = _____
19. 9 × 9 = _____
20. 5 × 7 = _____
21. 4 × 8 = _____

Name _____

Practice
Chapters 1–7

Cumulative Review

(Chapter 2 Lesson 5) Make a list or use any strategy to solve.

1. Chelsea sells flower bulbs to gardeners. She has 48 bulbs that can be packed in boxes of 8 or 4. How many ways can she pack the bulbs? _____

Boxes of 8:							
Boxes of 4:							

(Chapter 6 Lessons 3, 4 and 8) Multiply.

2. 3   3. 7   4. 4   5. 7   6. 9
   ×6   ×3   ×8   ×6   ×7

7. 8   8. 6   9. 3   10. 7   11. 9
   ×8   ×4   ×8   ×7   ×6

12. $7 \times 8 =$ _____   13. $8 \times 6 =$ _____
14. $7 \times 4 =$ _____   15. $5 \times 6 \times 0 =$ _____
16. $2 \times 3 \times 8 =$ _____   17. $1 \times 7 \times 8 =$ _____
18. $2 \times 4 \times 3 =$ _____   19. $2 \times 2 \times 7 =$ _____

(Chapter 7 Lessons 6 and 7) Find each quotient.

20. $15 \div 3 =$ _____   21. $10 \div 5 =$ _____
22. $25 \div 5 =$ _____   23. $36 \div 4 =$ _____
24. $35 \div 5 =$ _____   25. $24 \div 4 =$ _____
26. $21 \div 3 =$ _____   27. $15 \div 5 =$ _____

28. $3\overline{)27}$ 29. $4\overline{)28}$ 30. $5\overline{)20}$ 31. $3\overline{)9}$

Name _____

Practice 8-1

Exploring Solids

1. Color the figures with flat faces red.
2. Color the figures that roll blue.

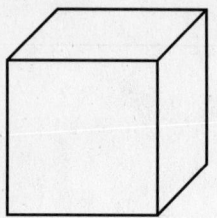
Cube

Sphere

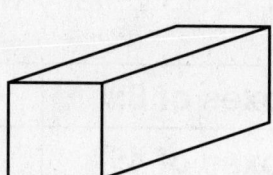
Rectangular Prism

Cone

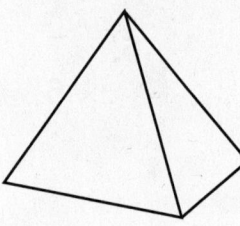
Pyramid

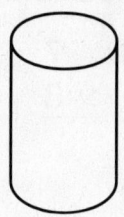
Cylinder

3. Which figures were colored twice? _____

Name the solid figure that each object looks like.

4.    5.    6.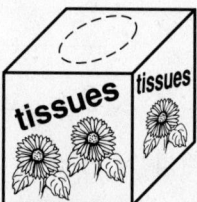

_____   _____   _____

7. What solid figure does a baseball look like? _____
8. What solid figure does a drum look like? _____
9. What solid figure does a book look like? _____

Name _____

Practice
8-2

Exploring Solids and Shapes

Name the shapes of the dotted faces on each solid figure.

1.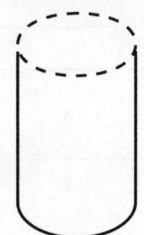
_____

2.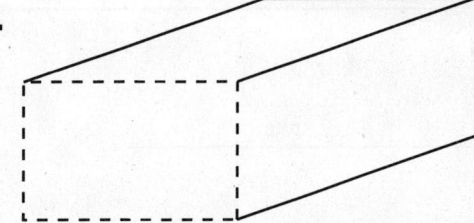
_____

3.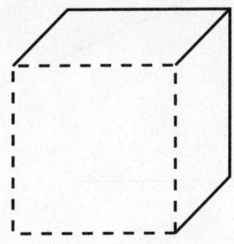
_____

4.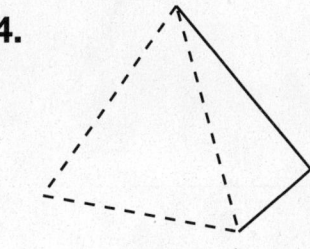
_____

Name the shape that each object looks like.

5.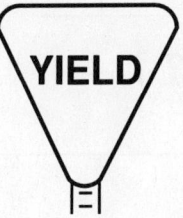
_____

6.
_____

7.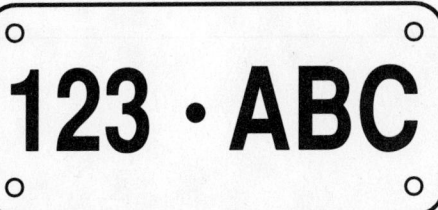
_____

8.
_____

9. How many sides does a rectangle have? _____

10. How many sides does a circle have? _____

Use with pages 324–325. **119**

Name _____

Practice 8-3

Lines and Line Segments

Write the name for each.

1. •————————————•

   _____

2.

   _____

3. •————————————→

   _____

4. (two intersecting lines forming an X)

   _____

5. ←————————————→

   _____

6. ←————————————•

   _____

7. How many endpoints does a line segment have? _____

8. How is a line segment like a ray? How is it different?
   _____
   _____

9. If two lines intersect, can they also be parallel? Explain.
   _____

10. Draw a line segment.

11. Draw 2 parallel lines.

Name _____

Practice 8-4

Exploring Angles

1. Write the number 1 by the right angle.
2. Write the number 2 by the angle that is less than a right angle.
3. Write the number 3 by the angle that is greater than a right angle.

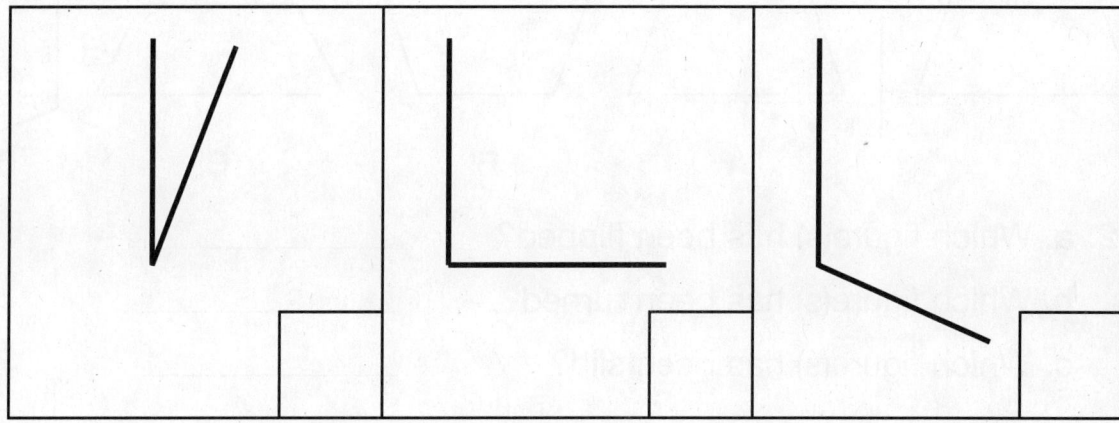

Write whether each angle is a right angle, less than a right angle, or greater than a right angle.

4.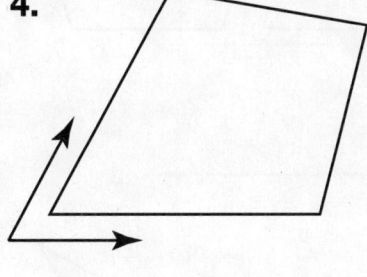

   _____
   _____

5.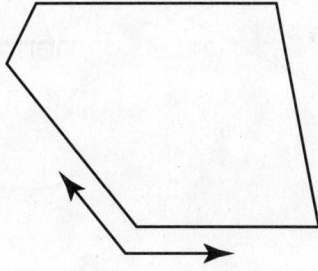

   _____
   _____

6.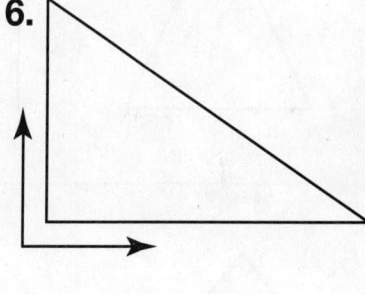

   _____
   _____

Write the number of right angles in each polygon.

7.

   _____

8.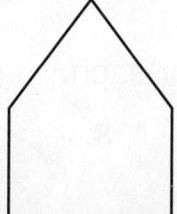

   _____

9.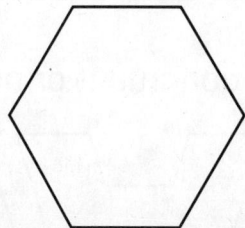

   _____

Use with pages 328–329. **121**

Name _____

Practice 8-5

Exploring Slides, Flips, and Turns

Congruent figures have the same size and shape.

1. Color the figures that are congruent to the first figure blue.

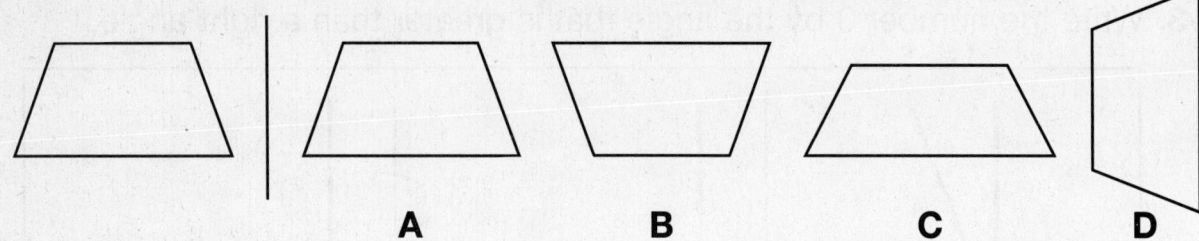

          A   B   C   D

2. a. Which figure(s) has been flipped? _____
   b. Which figure(s) has been turned? _____
   c. Which figure(s) has been slid? _____

Write slide, flip, or turn for each.

3.

4.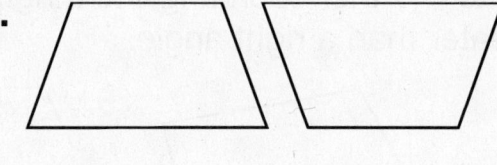

_____

5.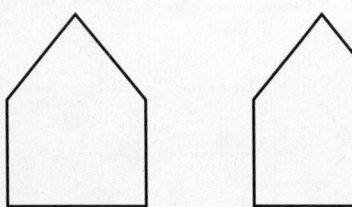

6.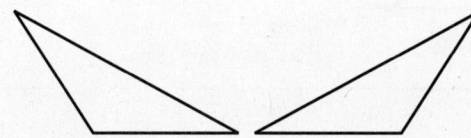

_____

Write congruent or not congruent for each.

7.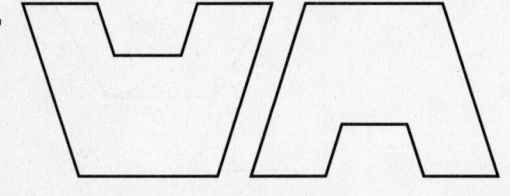

8.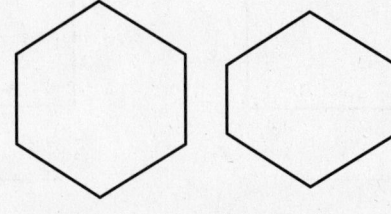

_____

Name _____

Practice 8-6

Exploring Symmetry

A figure has a line of symmetry if you could fold the figure so both parts match exactly. Some figures have more than one line of symmetry.

1. Draw lines of symmetry on each figure. Color the figures that have only one line of symmetry.

Does each figure appear to have a line of symmetry? Write yes or no.

2.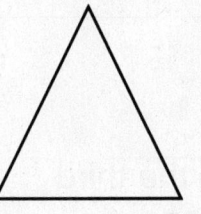

3.

_____

4.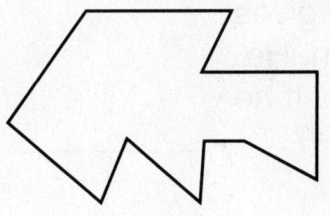

5.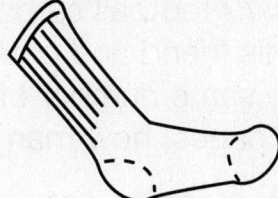

_____

Does each line appear to be a line of symmetry?
Write yes or no. If not, draw a correct line of symmetry.

6.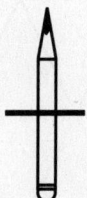

7.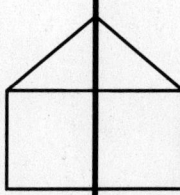

8.

_____

Use with pages 332–333.   **123**

Name _____

Practice 8-7

Analyze Strategies: Solve a Simpler Problem

See how many triangles you can find in this design.

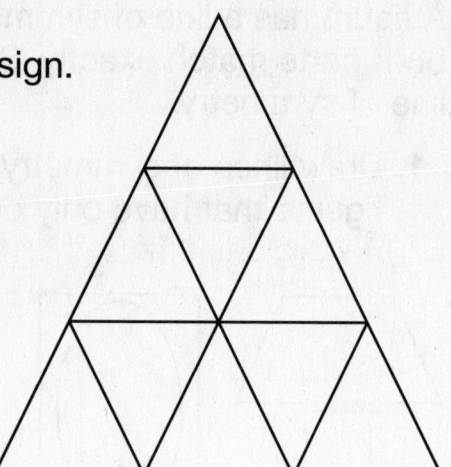

1. a. How many small triangles are in the design? _____

   b. How many medium-sized triangles are in the design? _____

   c. How many large triangles? _____

   d. How many triangles are there in all? _____

   e. What strategy did you use to solve the problem?

   _____
   _____

Use any strategy to solve each problem.

2. Sarah has three books to place together on her bookshelf. One book is red, another is blue, and the third is yellow. How many different ways can she arrange the books if she wants the blue book in the middle? _____

3. Bryan has 79 football cards in his collection. He gives seven to his friend and puts the rest in his album. He places the same number of cards on each page. If he uses nine pages, how many cards are on a page? _____

4. How many triangles can you find in this triangular design? _____

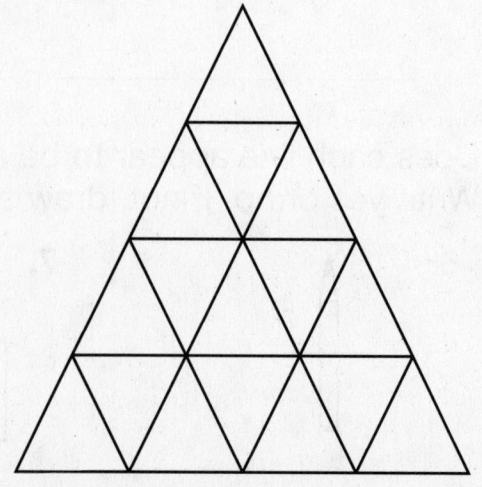

5. Four students are standing in a line. Ned is to the right of Helen. Carlos is the only one between Keith and Ned. Who is on the far left?

   _____

Name _____

Practice
Chapter 8
Section A

Review and Practice

Vocabulary Write true or false for each.

1. A cone has no faces.
   _____

2. A line segment is endless in both directions.
   _____

3. A right angle is an angle that forms a square corner.
   _____

4. A corner is where two or more edges meet.
   _____

(Lesson 1) Name the solid figure that each object looks like.

5.
_____

6.
_____

(Lesson 2) Write the number of sides that each shape has.

7.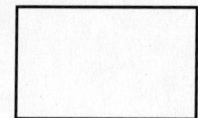
_____

8.
_____

9.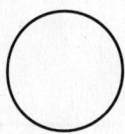
_____

(Lesson 5) Write slide, flip, or turn for each.

10.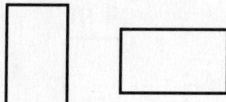
_____

11.
_____

12.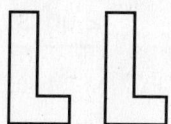
_____

(Lesson 6) Is each line a line of symmetry? Write yes or no.

13.
_____

14.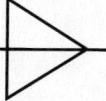
_____

15.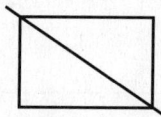
_____

(Mixed Review) Find each product or quotient.

16. $8 \times 8 =$ _____
17. $24 \div 3 =$ _____
18. $4 \times 7 =$ _____
19. $56 \div 7 =$ _____
20. $49 \div 7 =$ _____
21. $9 \times 3 =$ _____

Name _____

Practice 8-8

Exploring Perimeter

1. The perimeter is _____.

Find the perimeter of each.

2.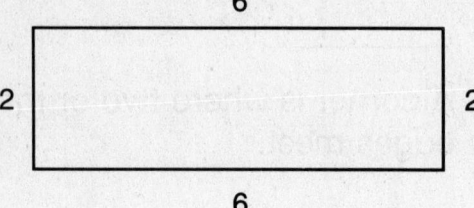

3.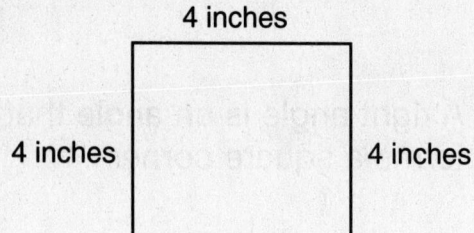

_____

_____

4.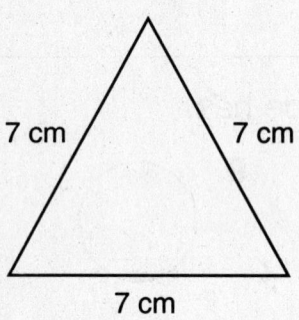

5.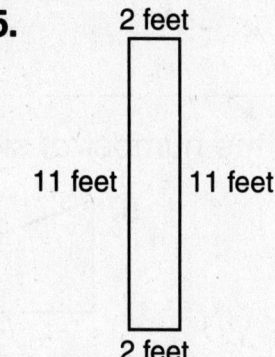

_____

_____

6.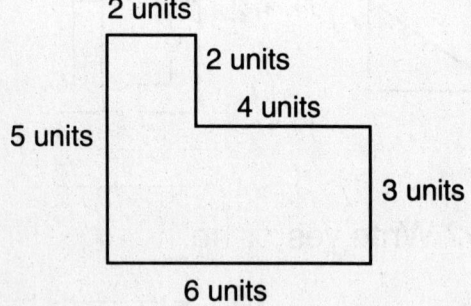

7.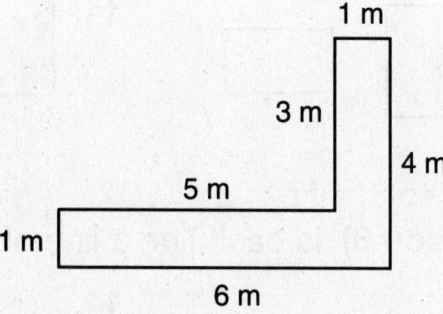

_____

_____

Use grid paper. Draw a shape with each perimeter.

8. 8 units   9. 12 units   10. 4 units

11. 20 units   12. 26 units   13. 11 units

126 Use with pages 340–341.

Name _____

Practice
8-9

Exploring Area

Find each area. Write your answer in square units.

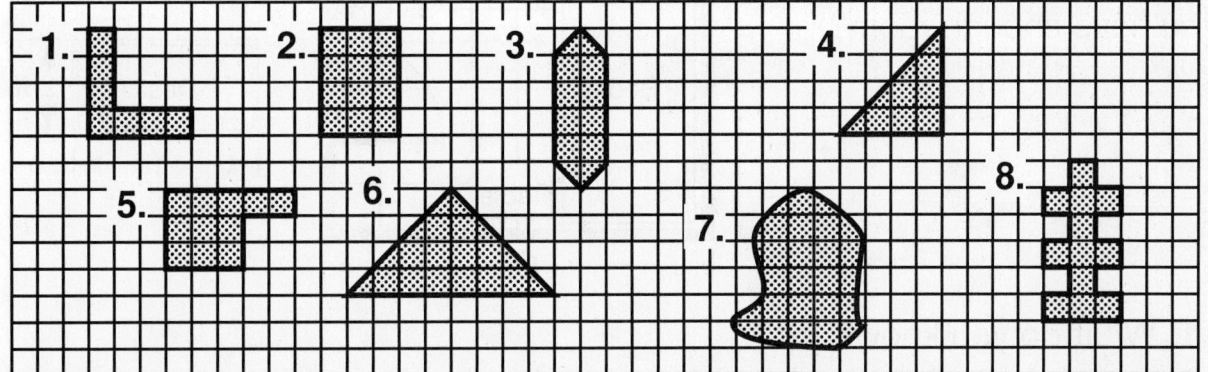

1. _____ 2. _____

3. _____ 4. _____

5. _____ 6. _____

7. _____ 8. _____

9. Use grid paper.

   a. Draw a rectangle with a perimeter that measures 10 units.

   b. What is the area of your rectangle?

   _____

   c. Draw a rectangle with the same perimeter but with a different area. What is the area of your rectangle?

   _____

10. a. What is the perimeter of the rectangle?

    _____

    b. What is the area of the rectangle? _____

    c. What happens to the perimeter if you halve each side?

    _____

    d. What happens to the area if you halve each side?

    _____

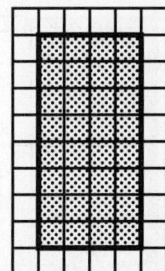

Use with pages 342–343.

Name _____

Practice 8-10

Decision Making

You want to move a desk into your bedroom. Do you have enough room?

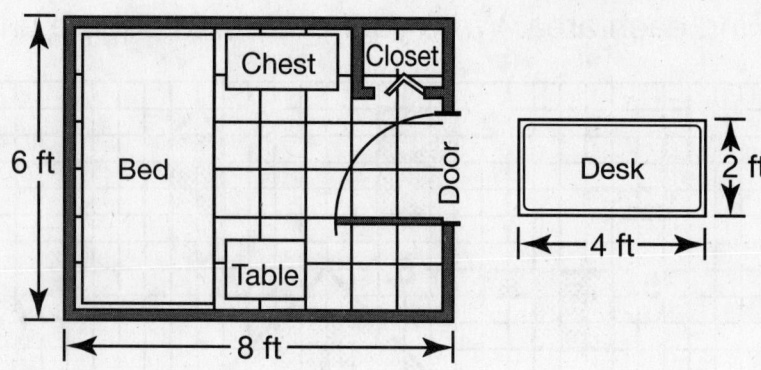

1. What do you know?
   _____

2. What do you need to decide?
   _____

3. What is the area of the desk?
   _____

4. What else do you have to consider other then the area of the desk?
   _____

5. Is there enough room for the desk?
   _____

Find the area of the room and the couch. Decide if the couch will fit in the room if no other furniture is moved.

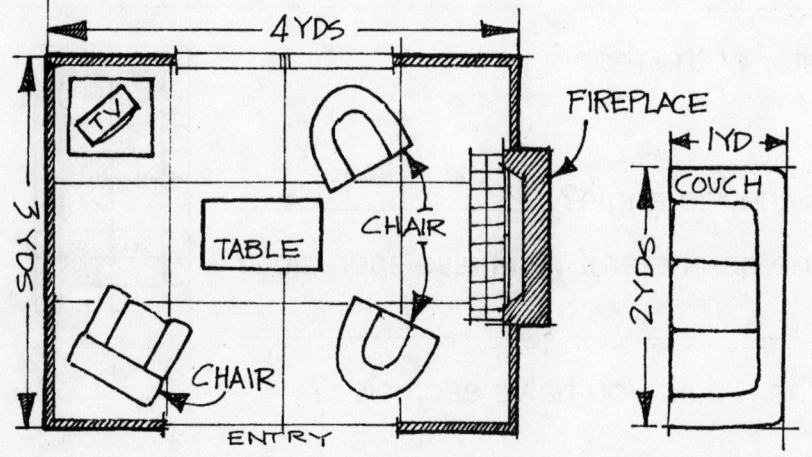

6. Area of room: _____

7. Area of couch: _____

8. Will the couch fit? _____

128 Use with pages 344–345.

Name _____

Practice 8-11

Exploring Volume

Write how many cubes are in each solid figure.

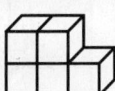

1. _____

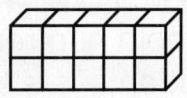

2. _____

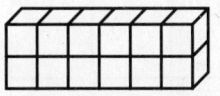

3. _____

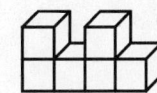

4. _____

Find the volume of each. You may use cubes to help.

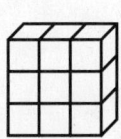

5. _____

6. _____

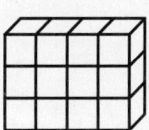

7. _____

8. _____

  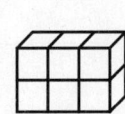 

9. Is there a difference in the volumes of these solid figures?
   Explain. _____

Use with pages 346–347.

Name _____

Practice 8-12

Coordinate Grids

Mr. Sanders has just begun teaching at a new school. This is a grid which Mr. Sanders drew to help him remember where each of his students is sitting.

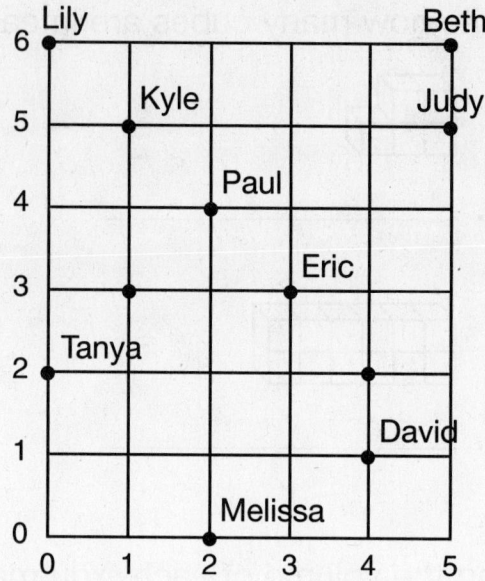

Write the ordered pair for each student's seat.

1. Kyle _____
2. David _____
3. Lily _____
4. Melissa _____
5. Beth _____
6. Tanya _____

Write the name of the student located at each ordered pair.

7. (3,3) _____
8. (5,5) _____
9. (0,2) _____
10. (2,4) _____
11. (5,6) _____
12. (2,0) _____

13. Are (0,2) and (2,0) at the same seat? Explain.

_____

14. To find Beth's seat from (0,0) how many spaces do you move to the right? _____

15. To find Paul's seat from (0,0) how many spaces do you move up? _____

16. Who is seated four places to the right of (1,5)? _____

17. Who is seated four places up from (0,2)? _____

18. Two new students join the class. Miranda sits at (1,3) and June sits at (4,2). Label these points on the grid.

Name _____

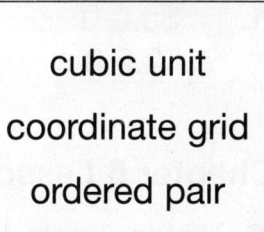

Practice
Chapter 8
Section B

Review and Practice

Vocabulary Choose the correct word to complete each sentence.

Word List
cubic unit
coordinate grid
ordered pair

1. A(n) _____ is a graph used to locate points.

2. The unit used to measure volume is a _____.

3. A pair of numbers used to locate a point on a grid is a(n) _____.

(Lessons 8 and 9) Find the area and perimeter of each shape.

4.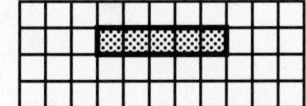

5.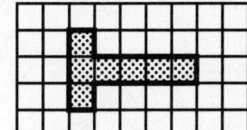

_____, _____   _____, _____

(Lesson 11) Find the volume of each.

6. 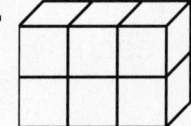   7. 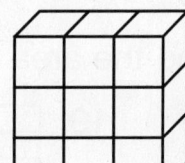   8.

_____   _____   _____

(Lesson 12) Write the ordered pair that locates each.

9. moon rock _____
10. movies _____
11. space food _____
12. photos _____
13. What is located at (3,2)? _____

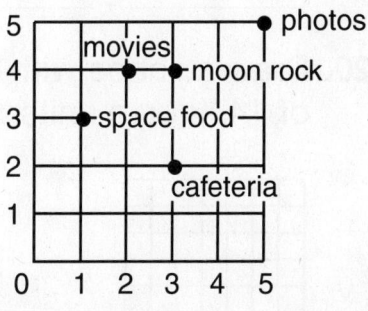

(Mixed Review) Find each sum.

14. 24 + 25 + 24 = _____   15. 33 + 43 = _____

16. 222 + 333 + 444 = _____   17. 67 + 29 = _____

Use with page 350.

Name _____

Practice
Chapters 1–8

Cumulative Review

(Chapter 4 Lesson 15) Find each difference.

1. $5.00
   − 2.50

2. $3.75
   − 1.58

3. $12.39
   − 9.81

4. $9.52
   − 6.99

(Chapter 6 Lesson 9) Solve. Use any strategy.

5. Vickie wants to fry enough sausage links so that each of her 7 guests gets to eat 4 links. The links come in packages of 6. How many packages must she buy? _____

(Chapter 7 Lessons 10 and 11) Find each quotient.

6. 18 ÷ 6 = _____
7. 16 ÷ 8 = _____
8. 21 ÷ 7 = _____
9. 63 ÷ 7 = _____
10. 56 ÷ 8 = _____
11. 27 ÷ 9 = _____
12. 54 ÷ 6 = _____
13. 63 ÷ 9 = _____

14. 8)64   15. 9)72   16. 6)36   17. 7)7

(Chapter 8 Lessons 8 and 9) Find the area and perimeter of each.

18.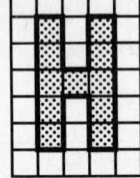

19.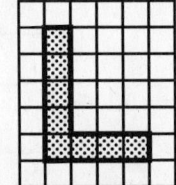

_____, _____   _____, _____

20. Draw a shape with an area of 14 square units.

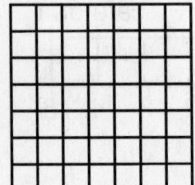

21. Draw a shape with a perimeter of 14 units.

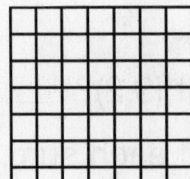

132 Use with page 355.

Exploring Multiplying Tens

Complete. You may use place-value blocks to help.

1. 5 groups of 7
   5 × ☐ ones = ☐ ones
   5 × 7 = ☐

2. 5 groups of 70
   5 × ☐ tens = ☐ tens
   5 × 70 = ☐

3. 5 × 1 ten = ☐ tens
   5 × 10 = ☐

4. 2 × 4 tens = ☐ tens
   2 × 40 = ☐

5. 3 × 5 tens = ☐ tens
   3 × 50 = ☐

6. 2 × 5 tens = ☐ tens
   2 × 50 = ☐

7. 3 × 6 tens = ☐ tens
   3 × 60 = ☐

8. 4 × 6 tens = ☐ tens
   4 × 60 = ☐

9. 7 × 1 ten = ☐ tens
   7 × 10 = ☐

10. 3 × 8 tens = ☐ tens
    3 × 80 = ☐

11. 4 × 4 tens = ☐ tens
    4 × 40 = ☐

12. 2 × 7 tens = ☐ tens
    2 × 70 = ☐

13. How can you use 7 × 6 to help you find 7 × 60?

_____

_____

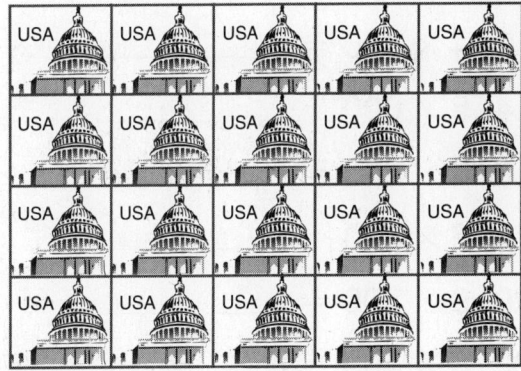

14. How many pennies are in 3 rolls? _____

15. How many stamps are on 5 sheets? _____

Name _____

Practice 9-2

Exploring Multiplication Patterns

Complete.

1. 6 × 7 ones = ☐ ones
   6 × 7 = ☐

2. 6 × 7 tens = ☐ tens
   6 × 70 = ☐

3. 6 × 7 hundreds = ☐ hundreds
   6 × 700 = ☐

4. 3 × 4 = ☐
   3 × ☐ = 120
   ☐ × 400 = 1,200

5. 2 × 4 = ☐
   ☐ × 40 = 80
   2 × 400 = ☐

6. 4 × ☐ = 20
   4 × 50 = ☐
   4 × ☐ = 2,000

7. 3 × 6 = ☐
   3 × ☐ = 180
   ☐ × 600 = 1,800

8. 7 × ☐ = 28
   7 × 40 = ☐
   ☐ × 400 = 2,800

9. 6 × 6 = ☐
   ☐ × 60 = 360
   6 × 600 = ☐

Find each product using mental math.

10. 3 × 90 = _____
11. 3 × 800 = _____
12. 4 × 400 = _____
13. 2 × 70 = _____
14. 5 × 600 = _____
15. 6 × 800 = _____
16. 3 × 300 = _____
17. 5 × 90 = _____
18. 6 × 300 = _____
19. 4 × 500 = _____
20. 9 × 200 = _____
21. 7 × 700 = _____
22. 8 × 400 = _____
23. 5 × 800 = _____

24. Can you use the basic fact 3 × 8 to find 3 × 800?

_____

25. Can you use 5 × 7 to find 5 × 700?

_____

134   Use with pages 362–363.

Estimating Products

Estimate each product.

1. 3 × 32 _____
2. 7 × 820 _____
3. 5 × 46 _____
4. 2 × 350 _____
5. 8 × 67 _____
6. 6 × 865 _____
7. 3 × 523 _____
8. 4 × 628 _____
9. 4 × 233 _____
10. 9 × 58 _____
11. 5 × 797 _____
12. 6 × 84 _____
13. 3 × 124 _____
14. 5 × 99 _____
15. 7 × 280 _____
16. 8 × 241 _____
17. 6 × 890 _____
18. 2 × 916 _____
19. 9 × 760 _____
20. 4 × 675 _____
21. 3 × 210 _____
22. 9 × 63 _____
23. 4 × 334 _____
24. 6 × 912 _____
25. 7 × 489 _____
26. 8 × 38 _____

27. Estimate the product of 6 and 34. _____
28. Estimate the product of 7 and 569. _____
29. Estimate the product of 9 and 435. _____
30. Estimate the product of 8 and 750. _____

31. Estimate to decide if 6 × 856 is greater than or less than 7 × 535. Explain.

_____

32. The product of 6 and another number is about 240. Give two numbers that make this sentence true. Explain.

_____

_____

Use with pages 364–365.

Name _____

Practice 9-4

Exploring Multiplication with Arrays

Complete the steps to find each product.

1. 3 × 14

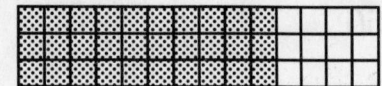

    a. 3 rows of 10
        3 × 10 = ☐

    b. 3 rows of 4
        3 × 4 = ☐

    c. ☐ + ☐ = ☐

    d. 3 × 14 = ☐

2. 2 × 26

    a. 2 rows of 20
        2 × 20 = ☐

    b. 2 rows of 6
        2 × 6 = ☐

    c. ☐ + ☐ = ☐

    d. 2 × 26 = ☐

3. 4 × 23 = _____

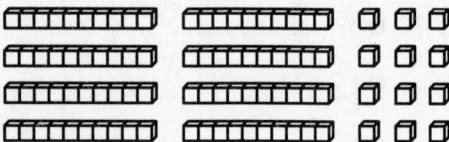

4. 5 × 13 = _____

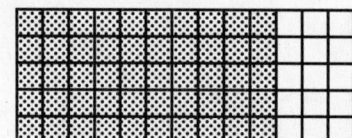

Find each product. You may use place-value blocks or grid paper to help.

5. 4 × 12 = _____   **6.** 6 × 13 = _____

7. 3 × 32 = _____   **8.** 4 × 17 = _____

9. 4 × 19 = _____   **10.** 2 × 47 = _____

11. 5 × 18 = _____   **12.** 3 × 28 = _____

13. 3 × 31 = _____   **14.** 2 × 39 = _____

Find the missing number. You may use grid paper or place-value blocks to solve.

15. 18 × _____ = 54   **16.** 12 × _____ = 84

17. 22 × _____ = 88   **18.** _____ × 19 = 57

19. 6 × 15 = _____   **20.** 5 × _____ = 70

136   Use with pages 366–367.

Name _____

Practice
Chapter 9
Section A

Review and Practice

(Lesson 1) Complete. You may use place-value blocks.

1. 5 × 1 ten = ☐ tens
   5 × 10 = ☐

2. 6 × 4 tens = ☐ tens
   6 × 40 = ☐

3. 8 × 3 tens = ☐ tens
   8 × 30 = ☐

4. 7 × 2 tens = ☐ tens
   7 × 20 = ☐

(Lesson 2) Complete.

5. 5 × 3 = ☐
   5 × ☐ = 150
   ☐ × 300 = 1,500

6. 6 × ☐ = 36
   ☐ × 60 = 360
   6 × ☐ = 3,600

Find each product using mental math.

7. 7 × 50 = _____
8. 9 × 600 = _____
9. 80 × 9 = _____
10. 400 × 8 = _____

(Lesson 3) Estimate each product.

11. 8 × 56 _____
12. 33 × 5 _____
13. 3 × 299 _____
14. 6 × 419 _____

15. Melissa collects stamps. She mounts them on pages that hold 63 stamps. About how many stamps will 6 pages hold? _____

(Lesson 4) Find each product. You may use place-value blocks or grid paper to help.

16. 6 × 12 = _____
17. 3 × 37 = _____
18. 5 × 27 = _____
19. 4 × 27 = _____

(Mixed Review) Add or subtract.

20. 361
    +839

21. 308
    −149

22. 917
    −579

23. 608
    + 55

Use with pages 368.   137

Practice 9-5

Multiplying: Partial Products

Find each product.

1. 15
    × 3
    ---
    1 5
    □□
    □□

2. 72
    × 2

    □
    1 4 0
    □□□

3. 21
    × 7

    □
    □□□
    □□□

4. 13
    × 6

    □□
    □□
    □□

5. 39
    × 7

    □□
    □□□
    □□□

6. 42
    × 6

    □□
    □□□
    □□□

7. 67
    × 7

    □□
    □□□
    □□□

8. 53
    × 5

    □□
    □□□
    □□□

9. 43 × 5 = _____

10. 64 × 3 = _____

11. 88 × 7 = _____

12. 39 × 4 = _____

13. 67 × 8 = _____

14. 37 × 6 = _____

15. 45 × 4 = _____

16. 69 × 2 = _____

17. 36 × 2 = _____

18. 84 × 5 = _____

19. 18 × 6 = _____

20. 23 × 9 = _____

21. Explain why 9 × 34 is the same as 270 + 36.

_____

22. How can you tell that 7 × 23 will be at least 3 digits?

_____

_____

23. Alexis says, "The product of 5 and 47 is less than 200." Is she right? Explain.

_____

Name _____

Practice 9-6

Multiplying 2-Digit Numbers

Find each product. Estimate to check.

1. 37 × 2
2. 43 × 7
3. 28 × 3
4. 56 × 5

5. 29 × 3
6. 72 × 6
7. 35 × 7
8. 92 × 6

9. 24 × 8
10. 53 × 5
11. 82 × 3
12. 47 × 6

13. 19 × 8
14. 37 × 9
15. 62 × 4
16. 90 × 7

17. 53 × 5 = _____
18. 37 × 3 = _____
19. 42 × 8 = _____
20. 38 × 7 = _____

21. Find the product of 17 and 9. _____

22. Find the product of 44 and 5. _____

23. Multiply 19 by 8. _____

24. Multiply 84 by 6. _____

25. Do you need to regroup ones to find the product of 42 and 3? Explain.

_____

26. Do you need to regroup to find the product of 34 and 3? Explain.

_____

27. How can you tell what the ones digit of the product of 38 × 7 will be without solving the whole problem?

_____

Name _____

Practice 9-7

Multiplying 3-Digit Numbers
Find each product. Estimate to check.

1. 542
   × 6

2. 374
   × 3

3. 722
   × 5

4. 256
   × 7

5. 346
   × 4

6. 117
   × 8

7. 612
   × 7

8. 739
   × 2

9. 513
   × 6

10. 757
    × 3

11. 198
    × 4

12. 209
    × 8

13. 127
    × 5

14. 508
    × 6

15. 138
    × 5

16. 377
    × 9

17. 4 × 311 = _____

18. 478 × 8 = _____

19. 491 × 5 = _____

20. 7 × 219 = _____

21. 9 × 106 = _____

22. 627 × 6 = _____

23. Multiply 7 and 524. _____

24. Find the product of 378 and 6. _____

25. How could you use mental math to find 5 × 306?
    _____
    _____

26. How could you use mental math to find 3 × 122?
    _____
    _____

Use with pages 378–379.

Name _____

Practice 9-8

Multiplying Money
Find each product.

1. $1.20 × 5

2. $0.65 × 7

3. $3.24 × 6

4. $1.75 × 5

5. $0.49 × 8

6. $3.19 × 4

7. $2.39 × 3

8. $4.12 × 5

9. $2.25 × 3

10. $1.52 × 6

11. $2.22 × 6

12. $4.33 × 7

13. 6 × $7.41 = _____

14. $2.29 × 4 = _____

15. $1.19 × 8 = _____

16. 9 × $0.79 = _____

17. $5.25 × 4 = _____

18. 7 × $3.50 = _____

19. What is the product of 5 and $7.44? _____

20. Multiply 6 and $0.72. _____

21. Is $0.32 the same amount as 32¢? _____

22. Mindy multiplied $1.37 and 4. She recorded $5.48. Is she correct? _____

23. If you bought 9 cans of juice for 72¢ each, would you spend more than $5.00? Explain.

_____

24. Ralph multiplied $2.69 and 5. He recorded $1345. Is he correct?

_____

Use with pages 380–381. **141**

Name _____

Practice 9-9

Mental Math

Find each product using mental math.

1. 42 × 3   2. 26 × 2   3. 14 × 6   4. 23 × 5

_____   _____   _____   _____

5. 32 × 8   6. 17 × 9   7. 37 × 3   8. 19 × 4

_____   _____   _____   _____

9. 21 × 6   10. 44 × 3   11. 53 × 4   12. 63 × 2

_____   _____   _____   _____

13. Multiply 6 and 47. _____

14. What is the product of 92 and 7. _____

15. If you know 30 × 4 = 120, how could you solve 36 × 4 mentally?

_____

16. If you know 30 × 3 = 90, how could you solve 29 × 3 mentally?

_____

17. What are two ways you could use mental math to find the product of 57 and 2?

_____

Name _____

Practice 9-10

Analyze Strategies: Make a Table

1. This summer, a new 20-story hospital was built downtown. Electricians worked quickly to put in wiring in the building. After one week, 4 floors had wiring. After two weeks, 8 floors had wiring. After three weeks, 12 floors had wiring.

   a. Fill in the table to show what you know.

Week	1	2	3	4	5
Floors Wired	4				

   b. What multiplication pattern can help you complete the table?

   _____

   _____

   c. If the electricians continued to work at the same speed, how many weeks did it take them to put in wire in all 20 floors? _____

2. If it takes Ginny 7 minutes to ride 1 mile on her bike, how long would it take her to ride 6 miles? _____

3. If Todd can throw 20 curve balls in one minute, how many curve balls could he throw in 4 minutes? _____

4. Shea is decorating a frame. She has 4 rubber stamps she could use. They are a leaf, a ladybug, a flower, and a bee. She wants to make a design with 2 rubber stamps. How many choices does she have? _____

5. Eduardo has a red shirt, a blue shirt, and a white shirt, black trousers and blue jeans. How many different outfits can he make? _____

Use with pages 386–387. **143**

Practice
Chapter 9
Section B

Name _____

Review and Practice

(Lessons 5–8) Find each product.

1. 43
    × 7

2. 23
    × 3

3. 93
    × 6

4. 62
    × 4

5. 308
    × 4

6. 611
    × 8

7. 980
    × 4

8. 237
    × 7

9. $6.18
    × 9

10. $1.23
    × 6

11. $0.11
    × 4

12. $4.56
    × 3

13. Sheila has 5 packets of raisins. Each packet contains 214 raisins. About how many raisins does Sheila have in all?

    _____

14. Jack buys 4 tickets to a concert. Each ticket costs $4.89. How much does Jack spend?

    _____

(Lesson 9) Use mental math to find each product.

15. $34 \times 5 =$ _____

16. $82 \times 3 =$ _____

17. $38 \times 4 =$ _____

18. $72 \times 4 =$ _____

(Lesson 10) Use any strategy to solve.

19. Kerim is saving money to buy a present. The first week he saves $1. The next week he saves $3. The third week he saves $5. If this pattern continues, how many more weeks will it be until he saves $25 in all? _____

(Mixed Review) Find each quotient.

20. $56 \div 8 =$ _____

21. $48 \div 6 =$ _____

22. $63 \div 9 =$ _____

23. $45 \div 5 =$ _____

Name _____

Practice 9-11

Exploring Division Patterns

Find the quotients. Use basic facts and place-value patterns to help you divide mentally.

1. 8 ones ÷ 2 = _____ ones

    8 ÷ 2 = _____

    8 tens ÷ 2 = _____ tens

    80 ÷ 2 = _____

    8 hundreds ÷ 2 =

    _____ hundreds

    800 ÷ 2 = _____

2. 9 ones ÷ 3 = _____ ones

    9 ÷ 3 = _____

    9 tens ÷ 3 = _____ tens

    90 ÷ 3 = _____

    9 hundreds ÷ 3 =

    _____ hundreds

    900 ÷ 3 = _____

Complete.

3. 7 ÷ 7 = _____

    70 ÷ _____ = 10

    _____ ÷ 7 = 100

5. 8 ÷ 4 = _____

    80 ÷ _____ = 20

    _____ ÷ 4 = 200

4. 8 ÷ 2 = _____

    _____ ÷ 2 = 40

    _____ ÷ 2 = 400

6. 10 ÷ 2 = _____

    100 ÷ _____ = 50

    _____ ÷ 2 = 500

Find each quotient using mental math.

7. 800 ÷ 2 = _____

9. 200 ÷ 4 = _____

11. 210 ÷ 7 = _____

8. 90 ÷ 9 = _____

10. 270 ÷ 3 = _____

12. 360 ÷ 6 = _____

13. How can you use 16 ÷ 4 = 4 to help you find 160 ÷ 4?

_____

Use with pages 390–391. **145**

Name _____

Practice 9-12

Estimating Quotients

Estimate each quotient.

1. 25 ÷ 6 _____
2. 35 ÷ 4 _____
3. 17 ÷ 4 _____
4. 29 ÷ 4 _____
5. 31 ÷ 8 _____
6. 19 ÷ 6 _____
7. 20 ÷ 3 _____
8. 14 ÷ 5 _____
9. 35 ÷ 6 _____
10. 39 ÷ 8 _____
11. 13 ÷ 6 _____
12. 65 ÷ 8 _____
13. 10 ÷ 3 _____
14. 11 ÷ 5 _____
15. 13 ÷ 4 _____
16. 73 ÷ 9 _____

17. Estimate the quotient of 25 ÷ 3. _____
18. Estimate the quotient of 41 ÷ 5. _____

19. What basic division fact can you use to help you estimate the quotient of 14 ÷ 5? Explain.

_____

_____

20. Is the quotient of 49 ÷ 6 greater than or less than 8? Explain.

_____

_____

21. Is the quotient of 53 ÷ 9 greater than or less than 6? Explain.

_____

_____

Name _____

Practice 9-13

Exploring Division with Remainders

Find each quotient and remainder. You may use counters to help you.

1. 2)13
2. 8)29
3. 5)33

4. 4)25
5. 3)17
6. 6)21

7. 7)18
8. 5)28
9. 6)55

10. 5)16
11. 7)47
12. 3)26

13. Catherine says, "If I have 19 strawberries, I can give myself and 3 friends each 5 strawberries." Do you agree or disagree?

_____

14. Kim says, "If I need 25 granny-squares for a quilt, I can knit 8 squares a week for 3 weeks." Do you agree or disagree?

_____

15. Stefan was packing books into boxes. He had 8 boxes that would each hold 4 books. Stefan had 33 books. How many would not fit into the boxes?

_____

16. Robin is putting photographs into an album. He can fit 7 photographs onto a page. The album has 7 pages and Robin has 53 photographs. How many will not fit in the album?

_____

Use with pages 394–395.

Name _____

Practice 9-14

Dividing
Find each quotient and remainder.

1. 2)15   2. 4)23   3. 8)56   4. 5)43

5. 6)25   6. 9)48   7. 6)56   8. 4)33

9. 42 ÷ 7 = _____   10. 70 ÷ 8 = _____
11. 51 ÷ 8 = _____   12. 26 ÷ 3 = _____
13. 22 ÷ 8 = _____   14. 61 ÷ 7 = _____
15. 35 ÷ 9 = _____   16. 48 ÷ 6 = _____
17. 47 ÷ 5 = _____   18. 34 ÷ 8 = _____

19. Divide 55 by 7. _____   20. Divide 66 by 8. _____
21. Divide 44 by 6. _____   22. Divide 33 by 4. _____
23. Divide 22 by 5. _____   24. Divide 88 by 9. _____

25. 12 volunteers will paint 4 walls. How many volunteers should work on each wall? _____

26. Suppose you want at least 15 rolls of film for your vacation. How many 4-roll packages should you buy? _____

27. How many traffic lights can you fill with a case of 24 light bulbs? (There are 3 lights on each traffic light.) _____

28. How many take-out boxes can you fill from a crate of 50 muffins if there are 6 muffins per take-out box? _____

29. Suppose 1 bottle of juice serves 5 people. How many bottles will you need for 27 people? _____

Use with pages 396–397.

Name _____

Practice 9-15

Decision Making

You are planning a race. You need a water station every 3 miles. How many water stations will you need if the race is:

1. 12 miles long? _____

2. 21 miles long? _____

3. 15 miles long? _____

4. 18 miles long? _____

5. 24 miles long? _____

6. 30 miles long? _____

7. 26 miles long? _____

8. 20 miles long? _____

9. There are 36 runners in your race. They must be divided into equal starting groups. Find 3 different ways to divide 36 runners into equal groups.

   a. _____ groups of _____ = 36

   b. _____ groups of _____ = 36

   c. _____ groups of _____ = 36

10. What if there are only 12 runners? Find 3 different ways to divide 12 runners into equal groups.

    a. _____ groups of _____ = 12

    b. _____ groups of _____ = 12

    c. _____ groups of _____ = 12

Use with pages 398–399.

Review and Practice

Vocabulary Underline the term that will complete the sentence correctly.

1. The (quotient, product) is the answer to a division problem.

2. The (quotient, remainder) is the number left over after dividing.

(Lesson 11) Use mental math to find each quotient.

3. 300 ÷ 6 = _____
4. 320 ÷ 8 = _____
5. 630 ÷ 7 = _____
6. 160 ÷ 4 = _____

7. Sarah's family is going on a 120-minute walk. They stop to rest 3 times. How often to they stop to rest?

_____

(Lesson 12) Estimate each quotient.

8. 31 ÷ 5 = _____
9. 46 ÷ 9 = _____
10. 19 ÷ 3 = _____
11. 52 ÷ 7 = _____

(Lessons 13 and 14) Find each quotient and remainder.

12. 2)9
13. 6)43
14. 4)29
15. 5)47

16. 69 ÷ 9 = _____
17. 58 ÷ 7 = _____

18. A bottle holds 9 ounces. How many bottles are needed to hold 57 ounces? Will all the bottles be full? Explain.

_____

_____

(Mixed Review) Add or subtract.

19. 135
    +222

20. 504
    −243

21. 379
    − 84

22. 803
    + 59

Name _____

Practice 10-7

Exploring Finding a Fraction of a Number

Complete.

1. To find $\frac{1}{4}$ of 12 divide 12 into _____ equal groups.

2. To find $\frac{1}{3}$ of 15 divide 15 into _____ equal groups.

Solve. You may use counters or draw a picture to help.

3. $\frac{1}{2}$ of 18 = _____

4. $\frac{1}{7}$ of 21 = _____

5. $\frac{1}{10}$ of 10 = _____

6. $\frac{1}{4}$ of 8 = _____

7. Find $\frac{1}{3}$ of 9. _____

8. Find $\frac{1}{4}$ of 20. _____

9. Find $\frac{1}{5}$ of 30. _____

10. Find $\frac{1}{6}$ of 24. _____

11. What fraction of the animals are:

    a. dogs? _____   b. cats? _____   c. birds? _____

12. Suppose an adult slept for $\frac{1}{4}$ of a 24-hour day. How many hours did the person sleep?

_____

Use with pages 426–427.

Name _____

Practice
10-8

Mixed Numbers

Write a mixed number for each.

1.

   _____

2.

   _____

3.

   _____

4.

   _____

5.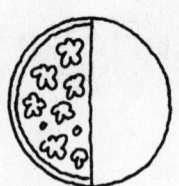

   _____

6.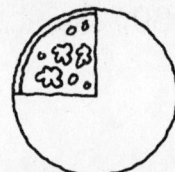

   _____

Answer each question.

7. Is there more or less than $1\frac{1}{4}$ pizzas? Explain.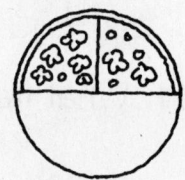

   _____

   _____

8. Leo said "$3\frac{3}{12}$ is the same as $3\frac{1}{4}$." Do you agree
   or disagree? Explain.

   _____

160   Use with pages 428–429.

Name _____

Practice
Chapter 10
Section B

Review and Practice

(Lesson 6) Write a fraction that tells what part of the set is circled.

1.  2.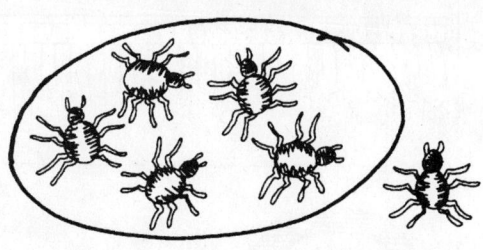

_____   _____

(Lesson 7) Solve. You may use counters or draw a picture to help.

3. Find $\frac{1}{4}$ of 24. _____   4. Find $\frac{1}{3}$ of 12. _____

5. Find $\frac{1}{5}$ of 20. _____   6. Find $\frac{1}{2}$ of 14. _____

7. Mitch has $18. He did put $\frac{1}{3}$ of the money in his savings account. How much did he put in his savings account? _____

(Lesson 8) Write a mixed number for each.

8.    9.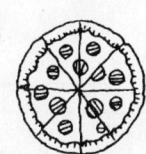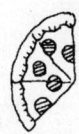

_____   _____

(Lesson 9) Find each sum or difference. You may use fraction strips or draw a picture to help.

10. $\frac{1}{6} + \frac{4}{6} =$ _____   11. $\frac{4}{5} - \frac{1}{5} =$ _____

12. $\frac{7}{9} - \frac{3}{9} =$ _____   13. $\frac{3}{8} + \frac{2}{8} =$ _____

(Mixed Review) Add or subtract.

14. 62   15. 98   16. 80   17. 82
    +33   −19   +73   −45

Use with page 434. **163**

Name _____

Practice 10-11

Exploring Length

Estimate each length. Then measure to the nearest inch.

1. 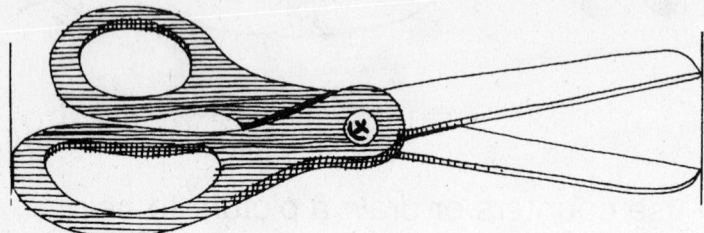 _____

2. 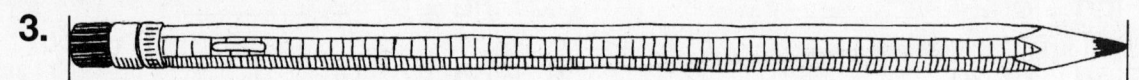 _____

3. _____

4.  _____

5. 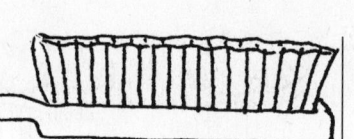 _____

6. Suppose you need at least 5 inches of wire for a project. Is this enough wire? _____

7. Measure the length of your thumb, your math book, and your arm. Write each measurement in order from greatest to least.

_____

8. Use a ruler. Draw a line to show each length.

   a. $2\frac{1}{2}$ inches

   b. 5 inches

   c. $6\frac{1}{4}$ inches

Name _____

Practice 10-12

Measuring to the Nearest $\frac{1}{2}$ Inch and $\frac{1}{4}$ Inch

Measure the length of each object to the nearest $\frac{1}{2}$ inch.

1.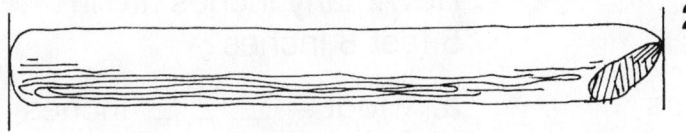

2.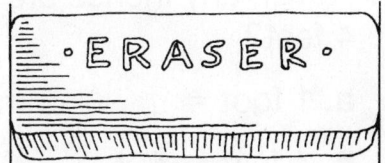

_____   _____

3.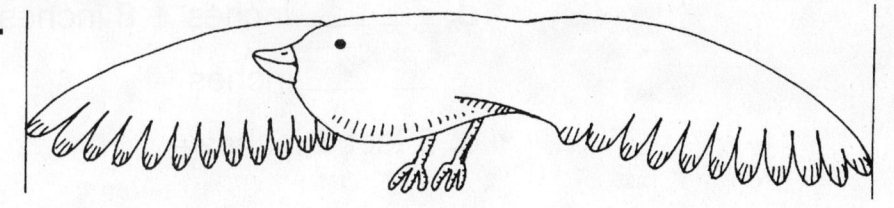

_____

Measure the length of each object to the nearest $\frac{1}{4}$ inch.

4.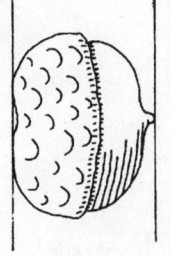

5.

_____   _____

6.

_____

7. You need to measure a pebble for a science project. Does it make more sense to measure to the nearest inch or $\frac{1}{2}$ inch?

_____

Use with pages 438–439. **165**

Name _____

Practice 10-13

Exploring Length in Feet and Inches

You can multiply to write measurements in feet as measurements in inches.

1. How many inches are in 4 feet?

   a. 1 foot = _____ inches
   b. 4 feet = 4 × _____ inches
   c. 4 feet = _____ inches

2. How many inches are in 5 feet 8 inches?

   a. 1 foot = _____ inches
   b. 5 feet = 5 × _____ inches
   c. 5 feet = _____ inches
   d. _____ inches + 8 inches = _____ inches
   e. 5 feet 8 inches = _____

Write each measurement in inches.

3. 4 feet 8 inches _____

4. 2 feet 11 inches _____

5. 5 feet 5 inches _____

6. 1 foot 9 inches _____

7. 6 feet 3 inches _____

8. 4 feet 4 inches _____

9. Does it make more sense to measure the length of your pencil in feet or inches? Explain.

   _____

   _____

10. Does it make more sense to measure the length of your classroom in feet or inches? Explain.

    _____

    _____

Name _____

Practice 10-14

Feet, Yards, and Miles

Compare. Write <, >, or =.

1. 1,760 yd ◯ 1 mile
2. 3 yd ◯ 8 ft
3. 5 ft ◯ 2 yd
4. 4,000 yd ◯ 2 mi
5. 2 mi ◯ 5,280 ft
6. 6 yd ◯ 2 ft
7. 40 in. ◯ 1 yd
8. 10 ft ◯ 3 yd
9. 1 mi ◯ 3,500 yd
10. 12 ft ◯ 4 yd
11. 20 in. ◯ 2 ft
12. 3 mi ◯ 5,000 yd
13. 4,500 ft ◯ 1 mi
14. 9 yd ◯ 3 ft

Choose an estimate for each.

15. length of your bed _____   a. 1 yard
16. distance a person jogs _____ b. 1 foot
17. height of a desk _____   c. 2 yards
18. length of a football _____   d. 1 mile

19. Would it make sense to measure the distance from your home to school in feet? Explain.

_____

_____

20. Would it make sense to measure a bicycle in feet? Explain.

_____

_____

Use with pages 442–443.

Name _____

Problem Solving 10-15

Analyze Strategies: Use Logical Reasoning

Use logical reasoning to solve.

1. Help Peter figure out which soccer teams finished in first, second, third, and fourth place. The Wings finished in third place. The Hawks beat the Eagles and the Wings. The Tigers finished in last place.

   _____

2. Ramon, Max, Jenna, and Maya are all on the same soccer team. Max is the youngest. Maya is older than Ramon. Jenna is 10 years old. If each player is either 9, 10, 11, or 12 years old, how old is each person?

   _____

Use any strategy to solve.

3. Sean, Sharon, Ali, and Marie all have scored goals this season. Sharon has scored more goals than Ali and Sean. Sean has scored fewer goals than the three other players. Sharon has scored fewer goals than Marie. Order the players from greatest number of goals scored to fewest.

   _____

4. I am an even number between 20 and 30. The sum of my tens digit and my ones digit is 6. What number am I? _____

5. I am an odd number between 50 and 60. The sum of my tens digit and my ones digit is 10. What number am I? _____

6. Mickey has 5 coins. The total value of the coins is $0.60. He doesn't have any pennies and only has 1 nickel. What coins does Mickey have?

   _____

7. I am a number between 10 and 20. The difference between my digits is 0. What number am I? _____

Name _____

Practice
Chapter 10
Section C

Review and Practice

Vocabulary Write true or false for each statement.

1. Kevin can walk 1 mile in 1 second. _____
2. This paper is about 1 foot in length. _____

(Lesson 11) Measure the length of the object to the nearest inch.

3. _____

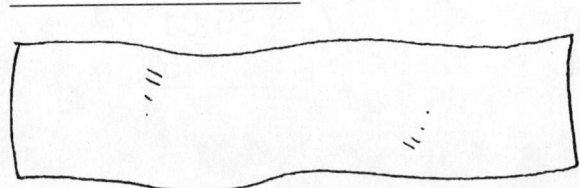

(Lesson 12) Measure the length of the object to the nearest $\frac{1}{4}$ inch.

4. _____

(Lesson 13) Write each measurement in inches.

5. 8 feet
6. 3 feet
7. 2 feet

(Lesson 14) Compare. Write <, >, or =.

8. 2 feet ◯ 22 inches
9. 2 yards ◯ 6 feet
10. 5 yards ◯ 140 inches
11. 3 miles ◯ 21,120 feet

(Lesson 15) Use any strategy to solve.

12. Freda has 9 coins worth $1. Two are quarters. None are pennies. There is 1 more nickel than there are dimes. What coins does Freda have?

_____

(Mixed Review) Multiply or divide.

13. $6 \times 2 =$ _____
14. $32 \div 8 =$ _____

Use with page 446. **169**

Name _____

Practice Chapters 1–10

Cumulative Review

(Chapter 4 Lesson 10) Subtract.

1. 673
  − 425

2. 315
  − 99

3. 830
  − 609

4. 749
  − 73

(Chapter 9 Lesson 8) Multiply.

5. $3.29
  × 3

6. $3.10
  × 4

7. $9.01
  × 5

(Chapter 9 Lesson 13) Find each quotient and remainder. You may use counters to help.

8. $3\overline{)13}$

9. $5\overline{)48}$

10. $7\overline{)59}$

11. $2\overline{)19}$

(Chapter 10 Lesson 2) Write the fraction of each figure that is shaded.

12. 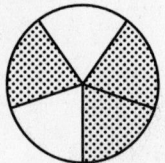 _____

13. 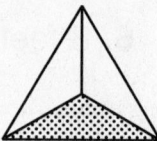 _____

(Chapter 10 Lesson 4) Compare. Write <, >, or =. You may use fraction strips to help.

14. $\frac{1}{4}$ ◯ $\frac{5}{8}$

15. $\frac{3}{6}$ ◯ $\frac{5}{12}$

16. $\frac{2}{4}$ ◯ $\frac{4}{8}$

17. $\frac{4}{5}$ ◯ $\frac{5}{10}$

18. $\frac{1}{2}$ ◯ $\frac{2}{3}$

19. $\frac{3}{4}$ ◯ $\frac{8}{12}$

(Chapter 10 Lesson 9) Find each sum or difference. You may use fraction strips or draw a picture to help.

20. $\frac{6}{8} + \frac{1}{8} =$ _____

21. $\frac{2}{5} + \frac{3}{5} =$ _____

22. $\frac{6}{9} - \frac{3}{9} =$ _____

23. $\frac{7}{8} - \frac{5}{8} =$ _____

Use with page 451.

Name _____

Practice 11-1

Exploring Tenths

Any number in tenths can be written as a fraction or as a decimal.

Complete the table.

	Grids	Fraction or Mixed Number	Decimal	Word Name
1.	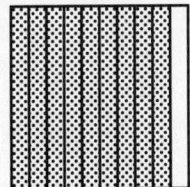		0.3	
2.				one and one tenth

Write the fraction and the decimal to name each shaded part.

3. 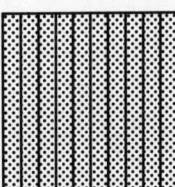 _____

4. 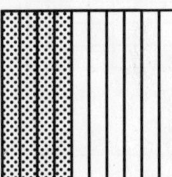 _____

Write each as a decimal.

5. eight tenths _____   6. $\frac{5}{10}$ _____

7. two and two tenths _____   8. $1\frac{6}{10}$ _____

9. Write each part of the circle as a fraction and a decimal.

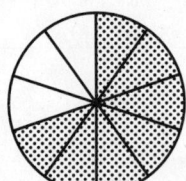

		Fraction	Decimal
a.	Shaded		
b.	Not shaded		

Use with pages 456–457. **171**

Name _____

Practice
11-2

Hundredths

Write the fraction and the decimal to name each shaded part.

1.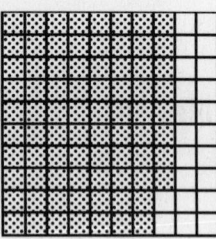

_____

2.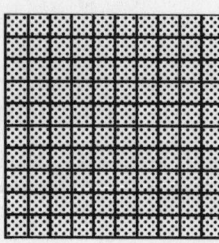

_____

3.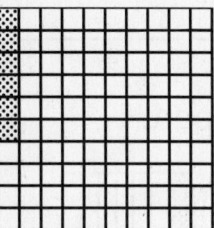

_____

4.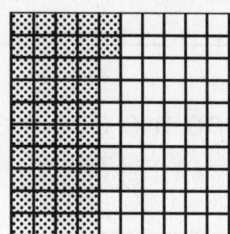

_____

Write each as a decimal.

5. seventeen hundredths _____
6. nine hundredths _____
7. one and three hundredths _____
8. $\frac{22}{100}$ _____
9. fifty-one hundredths _____
10. $\frac{1}{100}$ _____
11. $2\frac{65}{100}$ _____
12. $1\frac{99}{100}$ _____

13. Is 0.70 greater than, less than, or equal to 0.7? Explain.

_____

14. What is the value of each bold digit?

a. 0.8**4** _____

b. 1.**3**2 _____

c. **3**.59 _____

Name _____

Practice 11-3

Exploring Adding and Subtracting Decimals

You can add and subtract decimals using pencil and paper. You may use tenths grids to help.

1. Add 1.4 and 0.8.

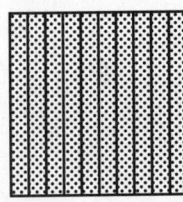 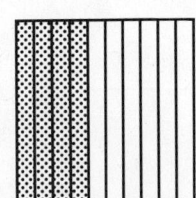 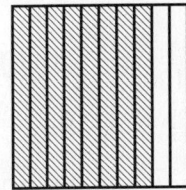

   a. Write the equation vertically in the space below. Line up the decimal points.

   b. Add tenths. Regroup if needed. Then add ones. What is the sum? _____

2. Subtract 1.6 from 2.5.

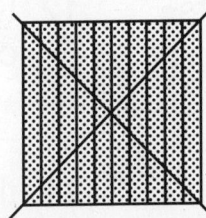 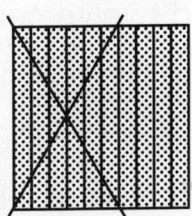 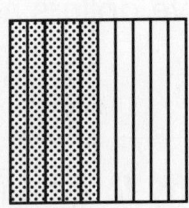

   a. Write the equation vertically in the space below. Line up the decimal points.

   b. Subtract tenths. Regroup if needed. Then subtract ones. What is the difference? _____

Find each sum or difference. You may use tenths grids to help.

3. 3.3   4. 1.9   5. 8.6   6. 6.2
   + 2.2   + 4.5   − 3.4   − 4.8

7. 0.7   8. 2.2   9. 5.8   10. 1.5
   + 0.3   − 1.9   − 0.7   + 1.6

Use with pages 460–461.

Name _____

Practice 11-4

Connecting Decimals and Money

Write each as a money amount.

1. $\frac{73}{100}$ of $1.00 _____

2. $\frac{39}{100}$ of $1.00 _____

3. $1\frac{15}{100}$ of $1.00 _____

4. $\frac{51}{100}$ of $1.00 _____

5. $2\frac{27}{100}$ of $1.00 _____

6. $\frac{98}{100}$ of $1.00 _____

7. sixty-six cents _____

8. forty-two cents _____

9. one dollar and ninety-one cents _____

10. three dollars and three cents _____

11. five dollars and twelve cents _____

12. two dollars and eighty-eight cents _____

13. fifty-four hundredths of $1.00 _____

14. three and thirty-seven hundredths of $1.00 _____

15. Complete the table.

		Fraction of $1.00	Decimal Part of $1.00
a.	$0.74		
b.	$0.02		
c.	$0.19		

174 Use with pages 462–463.

Name _____

Practice 11-5

Decision Making

You've decided to purchase a get-well gift for a friend who is ill. You want to go to the local mall to shop for the gift. Your goal is to find the perfect present and to be home by 5:00 P.M. You are bringing $10.00 with you. Below is a copy of the bus schedule for the bus which will take you to the mall. The bus stops on Carey Ave. right outside your house.

Leave Carey Ave.	Arrive Milford Mall	Leave Milford Mall	Arrive Carey Ave.
2:00 P.M.	2:15 P.M.	3:15 P.M.	4:00 P.M.
4:00 P.M.	4:15 P.M.	4:30 P.M.	4:45 P.M.

1. What information does the schedule give you?

   _____

   _____

2. When is the latest time you could leave the mall in order to get home on time?

   _____

   _____

3. How long does it take the bus to get to the mall from your bus stop on Carey Ave.? _____

4. If the one-way bus fare is $0.50, how much spending money do you actually have?

   _____

5. You buy a shirt for your friend. It costs $8.00. How much money do you have left over to buy a snack? (Don't forget about the bus fare!)

   _____

6. A muffin costs $0.60. Do you have enough money to buy one for your snack? _____
   Could you buy two muffins?

   _____

Use with pages 466–467. **175**

Name _____

Practice
Chapter 11
Section A

Review and Practice

Vocabulary Write true or false for each.

1. 85 cents is 85 tenths of a dollar. _____

2. A decimal uses place value and a decimal point to show tenths, hundredths, and so on. _____

3. The symbol used to separate ones from tenths in decimals is a comma. _____

(Lessons 1 and 2) Write the fraction and the decimal to name each shaded part.

4.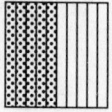

_____ ; _____

5.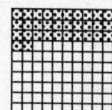

_____ ; _____

6.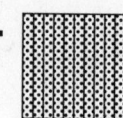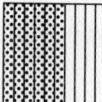

_____ ; _____

Write each as a decimal.

7. twenty-nine hundredths _____

8. $5\frac{3}{100}$ _____

9. two and four tenths _____

10. $\frac{8}{10}$ _____

(Lesson 3) Find each sum or difference. You may use tenths grids to help.

11. 3.8
    + 5.4

12. 8.3
    − 6.5

13. 2.6
    + 3.4

14. 8.5
    − 5.8

15. 4.7
    + 8.6

(Lesson 4) Write each as a money amount.

16. $\frac{16}{100}$ of $1.00 _____

17. $3\frac{29}{100}$ of $1.00 _____

(Mixed Review) Complete each number sentence.

18. 18 + _____ = 29

19. 57 − _____ = 21

20. _____ × 6 = 54

21. 56 ÷ _____ = 7

Name _____

Practice 11-6

Exploring Centimeters and Decimeters

1. Write 1 cm below the item that measures 1 cm. Write 1 dm below the item that measures 1 dm.

   a. 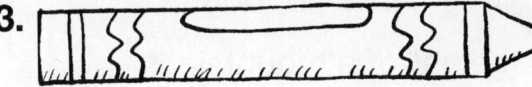   b.

   _____   _____

Estimate the length of each object. Then measure to the nearest centimeter.

2.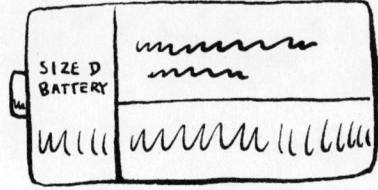

   estimate _____

   actual _____

3.

   estimate _____

   actual _____

Choose the best estimate for each.

4.

   a. 5 cm _____
   b. 1 dm

5.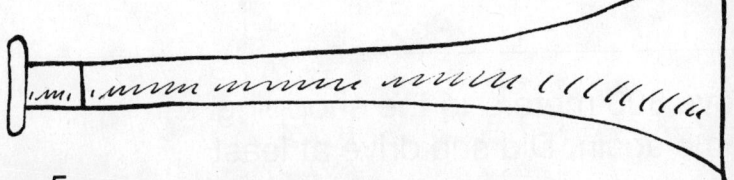

   a. 5 cm _____
   b. 1 dm

Use with pages 470–471. **177**

Name _____

Practice 11-7

Meters and Kilometers

Match each with its estimate.

1. length of a hiking trail _____   a. 30 cm
2. width of a frying pan _____   b. 2 kilometers
3. height of a chimney _____   c. 3 m

Write whether you would measure each in cm, m, or km.

4. length of a nail _____
5. length of a large table _____
6. length of a hot dog _____
7. height of a mountain _____
8. length of a van _____
9. distance of a 20-minute train ride _____
10. depth of a lake _____
11. length of the Mississippi River _____
12. length of a highway bridge _____

Answer each and explain your answers.

13. Is a 87-cm rug longer or shorter than a 1-meter rug? Explain.

_____

14. Is a 300-cm-long sofa longer or shorter than a meter? Explain.

_____

15. Suppose your mom drove 800 meters to the shopping mall and then drove home again. Did she drive at least one kilometer? Explain.

_____

178   Use with pages 472–473.

Name _____

Practice 11-8

Compare Strategies: Use Objects and Draw a Picture

Use any strategy to solve.

1. A bus starts off on its route. At the first stop 18 passengers get on. At the second stop 10 more board, but 2 get off. At the third stop 3 passengers get on and 1 passenger gets off. How many passengers are on board when the bus arrives at the fourth stop? _____

2. The same bus departed the terminal at 10:00 A.M. It arrived at the first stop 20 minutes later. It was delayed at this stop for 2 minutes. It took another 10 minutes for the bus to arrive at the second stop. At what time did the bus arrive at the second stop? _____

3. The same bus arrived at the third stop at 10:45. How much time went by between the time it arrived at the second stop and the time it arrived at the third stop? _____

4. Kim, Lisa, Ellen, and Martin have a jump rope contest. The jumper with the fewest misses wins. Martin wins with only 5 misses. Ellen has 3 more misses than Martin. Kim misses twice as many times as Ellen. Lisa has 2 fewer misses than Ellen. Can you give the scores for Ellen, Kim, and Lisa? Who came in second?

_____

5. Some students are making a chart to show how many students in the class were born in each month of the year. There are 22 students in the class. They find out that 1 student was born in January. Three times that many students were born in February. The months of March, April, September and October each had one less birth than the month of February. The rest of the students were born in the summer months. How many students had summer birthdays? _____

Use with pages 474–475. **179**

Name _____

Practice
Chapter 11
Section B

Review and Practice

Vocabulary. Choose the best word or words to complete each sentence. Use each word once.

| meter | kilometer | centimeter | decimeter |

1. A _____ is a metric unit equal to 1,000 meters.
2. A _____ is a metric unit equal to 10 _____s.
3. A _____ is a metric unit equal to 100 centimeters.

(Lesson 6) Match each with its estimate.

_____ 4. 1 m   a. width of an audio cassette tape
_____ 5. 1 dm   b. length of a pencil
_____ 6. 1 cm   c. height of your teacher's desk

(Lesson 7) Write whether you would measure each in cm, m, or km.

7. a car trip _____   8. length of a marathon _____
9. length of a car _____   10. width of a book _____
11. height of a dog _____ 12. height of a flag pole _____

(Lesson 8) Solve. Use any strategy.

13. A shelf at the grocery store had 15 loaves of bread on it. One shopper buys 3 loaves, another buys 5 loaves. The stock person restocks the shelf with 10 more loaves, then 3 more shoppers each buy 2 loaves. How many loaves of bread are on the shelf? _____

14. Maxine rode the elevator to the third floor, where she got off. She then climbed up 2 flights of stairs and got back on the elevator. She took the elevator down 3 floors. What floor is she now on? _____

(Mixed Review) Find each product.

15. 2 3   16. 4 5   17. $ 3 . 1 4   18. 8 2 2
    × 5   × 6   ×   9   ×   3

180 Use with page 476.

Name _____

Practice
Chapters 1–11

Cumulative Review

(Chapter 3 Lesson 10) Solve. Use any strategy.

1. The sum of 2 numbers is 61. The numbers are 5 apart. What are they? _____

2. The difference of 2 numbers is 10. The sum of the numbers is 14. What are they? _____

(Chapter 4 Lesson 11) Find each difference.

3. 807
  − 29

4. $306
  − 168

5. 900
  − 824

(Chapter 9 Lesson 14) Find each quotient and remainder.

6. 7)60   7. 8)56   8. 3)14   9. 5)32

(Chapter 10 Lesson 6) Write a fraction to tell what part of each set is circled.

10.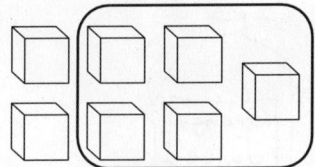

11.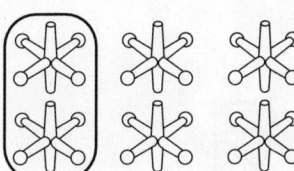

12.

_____   _____   _____

(Chapter 11 Lesson 3) Find each sum or difference.

13. 3.6
   + 2.3

14. 9.4
   − 6.8

15. 0.9
   + 7.7

16. 9.9
   − 1.6

(Chapter 11 Lesson 4) Write each as a money amount.

17. $\frac{26}{100}$ of $1.00 _____

18. $4\frac{53}{100}$ of $1.00 _____

19. three dollars and five cents _____

20. seventy-two hundredths of $1.00 _____

Name _____

Practice 12-1

Exploring Capacity: Customary Units

Complete.

1. _____ cups = 1 pint
2. 4 cups = _____ pints = _____ quart
3. _____ cups = 8 pints = _____ quarts = 1 gallon

Circle the best estimate for each.

4.

a. 1 cup
b. 1 quart
c. 1 pint

5.

a. 1 cup
b. 1 pint
c. 1 gallon

6.

a. 1 quart
b. 1 pint
c. 1 gallon

7.

a. 1 pint
b. 1 quart
c. 1 cup

8.

a. 1 pint
b. 1 quart
c. 1 gallon

9.

a. 1 cup
b. 1 quart
c. 1 gallon

Compare. Use <, >, or =.

10. 6 pints ◯ 1 gallon
11. 2 pints ◯ 3 cups
12. 2 quarts ◯ 4 pints
13. 16 cups ◯ 3 quarts

14. Suppose you want to make pudding. The recipe calls for 4 cups of milk. You have 1 quart. Do you have enough milk to make the recipe? Explain.

_____

Name _____

Practice 12-2

Measuring Capacity: Metric Units

Circle the better estimate for each.

1.
   a. 1 mL
   b. 1 L

2.
   a. 300 mL
   b. 300 L

3.
   a. 10 mL
   b. 10 L

4.
   a. 400 mL
   b. 400 L

5.
   a. 2 mL
   b. 2 L

6.
   a. 500 mL
   b. 500 L

7. Does a jar of honey hold about 600 mL or 600 L? _____

8. Does a plastic jug of milk hold about 3 mL or 3 L? _____

9. Suppose you estimated that you have made about 2 liters of lemonade. How could you check your estimate?

_____

_____

_____

10. What kind of container might hold many liters of water?

_____

Use with pages 488–489.

Name _____

Practice 12-3

Exploring Weight: Customary Units

Compare. Use <, >, or =.

1. 16 ounces ◯ 1 pound
2. 1 ounce ◯ 1 pound
3. 18 ounces ◯ 1 pound
4. 12 ounces ◯ 1 pound

Circle the better estimate for each.

5.
a. 11 oz
b. 11 lb

6.
a. 2 oz
b. 2 lb

7.
a. 7 oz
b. 7 lb

Write whether each is less or more than a pound.

8.
_____

9.
_____

10.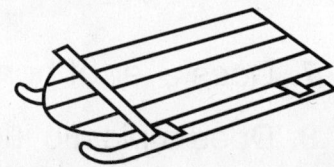
_____

11. Suppose a dog weighs 8 pounds. How many ounces does it weigh? _____

12. Suppose a person's brain weighs about 3 pounds. How many ounces does it weigh? _____

13. Complete the table.

Ounces	16	32		64	80	96
Pounds	1	2				

184 Use with pages 490–491.

Name _____

Practice 12-4

Grams and Kilograms

Circle the better estimate for each.

1.
   a. 2 g
   b. 2 kg

2.
   a. 560 g
   b. 560 kg

3.
   a. 15 g
   b. 15 kg

4.
   a. 100 g
   b. 100 kg

5.
   a. 4 g
   b. 4 kg

6.
   a. 50 g
   b. 50 kg

7. an 8-year-old boy
   a. 30 g
   b. 30 kg

8. a china cup
   a. 350 g
   b. 350 kg

9. a pen
   a. 5 g
   b. 5 kg

9. Remy says, "The number of grams in 2 kilograms is 2 × 1,000." Do you agree or disagree? Explain.

_____

_____

10. Which is heavier, a 3-kg rock or a 2,800-g rock? Explain.

_____

_____

Use with pages 492–493. **185**

Name _____

Practice 12-5

Temperature

Write the temperature using °C or °F.

1.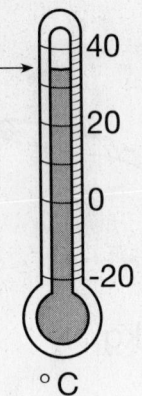
°C

2.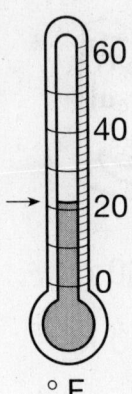
°F

3.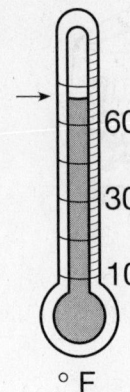
°F

_____

4.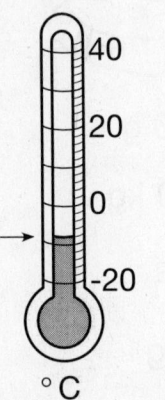
°C

5.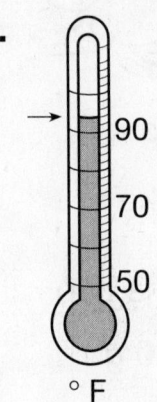
°F

6.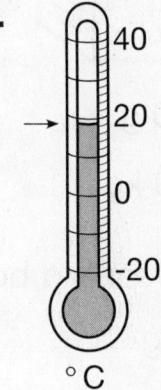
°C

_____

Circle the better estimate for each.

7.
a. 6°F
b. 68°F

8.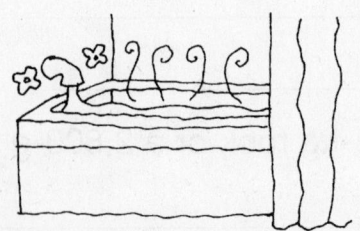
a. 7°C
b. 37°C

9.
a. 0°C
b. 20°C

10. Suppose it is 0°C outside. Should you wear a jacket?

_____

Decision Making

You are going on a backpacking trip. This is what you plan to take.

Item	Weight
backpack	3 lb
3 sweaters	1 lb each
1 canteen of water	2 lb 8 oz
2 pairs of pants	8 oz each
2 mess kits	8 oz each
3 flashlights	1 lb each
1 camera	2 lb
1 tape player	1 lb
4 cassette tapes	2 oz each
socks, t-shirts, etc.	2 lb

1. What will the total weight of your backpack be when you pack all of these items?

2. If you needed to make your pack 2 lb lighter, which items would you remove? Why?

3. If you had room in your pack for 3 lb more, what would you include? (Estimate the weight of the item if it is not on the list.)

Name _____

Practice
Chapter 12
Section A

Review and Practice

(Lessons 1 and 2) Circle the best estimate for each.

1.
   a. 1 pint
   b. 1 quart
   c. 1 gallon

2.
   a. 2 mL
   b. 2 L

3.
   a. 1 cup
   b. 1 gallon
   c. $\frac{1}{2}$ gallon

(Lessons 3 and 4) Circle the better estimate for each.

4.
   a. 14 oz
   b. 14 lb

5.
   a. 2 g
   b. 2 kg

6.
   a. 18 kg
   b. 1,800 kg

(Lesson 5) Write the temperature using °C or °F.

7.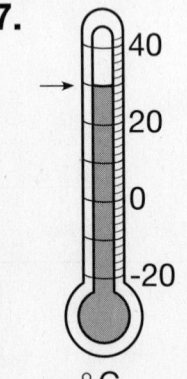
   °C
   _____

8.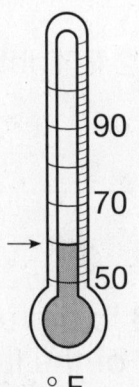
   °F
   _____

9.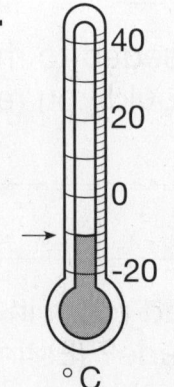
   °C
   _____

(Mixed Review) Add or subtract.

10. 318
    − 109

11. 825
    + 117

12. 700
    − 283

13. 421
    − 89

Name _____

Practice 12-7

Exploring Likely and Unlikely

1. Match each statement on the left with the best answer on the right.

   a. There will be no Wednesday next week.   Certain

   b. There will be clouds in the sky tomorrow.   Unlikely

   c. It will snow in Florida this year.   Impossible

   d. The desert will be hot this summer.   Likely

Write whether each is impossible, possible, or certain.

2. An elephant will learn how to fly. _____

3. Many trees will lose their leaves this fall. _____

4. A person is sleeping somewhere. _____

Write whether each is likely or unlikely.

5. The 6 o'clock news on TV will start late today. _____

6. Milk will be served in school cafeterias. _____

7. Next week, all of the books in the library will be checked out. _____

8. Your hair will be the same color in five years. _____

9. Students in your class will do some homework tonight. _____

10. It will rain daisies and roses tomorrow. _____

11. Heather said, "It is likely that flowers will bloom this spring." Do you agree or disagree? Explain.

    _____

    _____

Use with pages 500–501. **189**

Name _____

Practice 12-8

Exploring Predictions

1. Look at the spinner. List the possible outcomes of a spin. Complete the predictions with *more, fewer, all,* or *no.*

	Possible Outcomes	Predictions
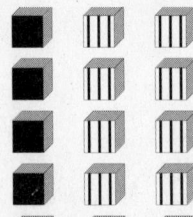		The pointer will land on dots _____ times. It will land on stripes _____ times.

Suppose you put these cubes in a bag. Predict which cubes you are more likely to pull out.

2.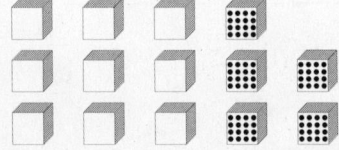

_____

3.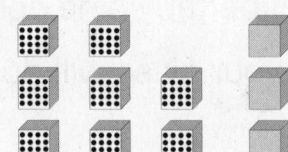

_____

4.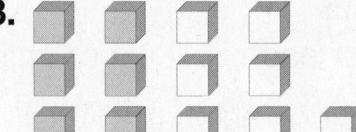

_____

5.

_____

6. Would it be easier to guess the month or the day of the week that someone was born? Explain.

_____

_____

190 Use with pages 502–503.

Name _____

Practice 12-9

Exploring Probability

Complete each sentence with a fraction that shows probability.

1. 3 out of 8 students are wearing blue shirts. The probability that a student is wearing a blue shirt is $\frac{\square}{8}$.

2. 2 out of 8 students are wearing red shirts. The probability that a student is wearing a red shirt is $\frac{\square}{8}$.

3. 2 out of 8 students are wearing green shirts. The probability that a student is wearing a green shirt is $\frac{\square}{8}$.

4. 1 out of 8 students is wearing a yellow shirt. The probability that a student is wearing a yellow shirt is $\frac{\square}{8}$.

5.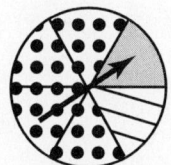

   a. grey: $\square$ out of 6 or $\frac{\square}{6}$

   b. striped: $\square$ out of 6 or $\frac{\square}{6}$

   c. dotted: $\square$ out of 6 or $\frac{\square}{6}$

6. 1 side of a plastic cube is orange, 2 sides are pink, and 3 sides are purple.

   a. If you toss the cube, which color is most likely to land face up? _____

   b. If you toss the cube, which color is least likely to land face up? _____

7. A contest has the following 15 prizes: 1 trip to Hawaii, 2 CD players, 3 pairs of hiking boots, 4 radios, and 5 posters. You have been told that you won one of the prizes.

   a. Which prize are you most likely to have won? _____

   b. Which prize are you least likely to have won? _____

Name _____

Practice 12-10

Exploring Fair and Unfair

1.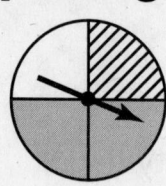

   a. ☐ out of 4 equal sections are gray.

   b. The probability of spinning gray is $\frac{\square}{4}$.

   c. Is spinning gray likely?
   _____

2.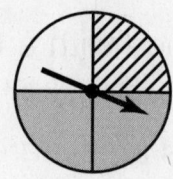

   a. ☐ out of 4 equal sections are white.

   b. The probability of spinning white is $\frac{\square}{4}$.

   c. Is spinning white likely?
   _____

3. Are the spinners shown in 1 and 2 fair? _____

Write whether each spinner is fair or unfair.

4.

   _____

5.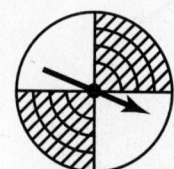

   _____

6.

   _____

7.

   _____

8. If there are 2 red cubes and 6 white cubes in a box, are the chances of picking a red cube likely, unlikely, or equally likely? Explain.

   _____

9. There are 3 green and 3 blue cubes in a box. Are the chances of picking a green cube likely, unlikely, or equally likely to picking a blue cube? Explain.

   _____

Use with pages 506–507.

Name _____

Practice
12-11

Analyze Strategies: Work Backward

Work backward or use any strategy to solve each problem.

1. Kim must be at the airport at 8:00 A.M. She needs 45 minutes to shower, dress, and eat breakfast. She needs 1 hour to drive to the airport. She wants to allow an extra 30 minutes for traffic. She needs 8 hours and 45 minutes of sleep the night before her trip. What time should she go to sleep?

_____

2. Jody said, "I am thinking of a number. If I add 24 to the number, then subtract 6, then add 12, and then multiply by 2, I end up with 84." What number did Jody start with? _____

3. Skyler has a large piece of blue fabric. She wants to make table napkins out of it. If each napkin requires 1 square foot of fabric, how many napkins can she make from the fabric? Use the drawing to help.

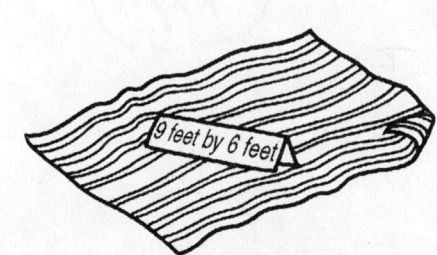

_____

4. Jason used the exercise machines at the gym. He worked on 2 machines for his arms. He skipped 5 arm exercises that he usually did because each of these machines was busy. Then he worked on his legs, using 6 machines. How many machines does Jason usually use?

_____

5. Derek used small rocks to border the garden. He used $\frac{1}{2}$ of the rocks to border the roses. Then he used 31 rocks to border the tulips and 25 to border the daffodils. He had 24 rocks left over. How many rocks did Derek start with?

_____

Name _____

Practice
Chapter 12
Section B

Review and Practice

Vocabulary Match each with its definition.

_____ 1. certain   a. able to happen
_____ 2. possible   b. a guess about what will happen
_____ 3. likely   c. sure to happen
_____ 4. prediction   d. probably will happen

(Lesson 8) Suppose you put these letters in a bag. Predict which letter you are more likely to pull out.

5.

6.

7.

_____   _____   _____

(Lesson 9) Complete.

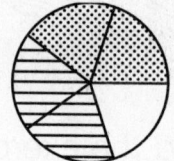

8. striped: _____ out of 5 or $\frac{\square}{5}$.

9. dotted: _____ out of 5 or $\frac{\square}{5}$.

10. white: _____ out of 5 or $\frac{\square}{5}$.

(Lesson 10) Write whether each spinner is fair or unfair.

11.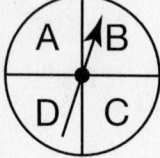

12.

13.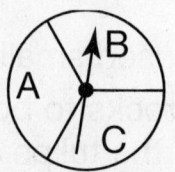

_____   _____   _____

(Mixed Review) Divide.

14. $3\overline{)19}$ 15. $5\overline{)49}$ 16. $8\overline{)47}$ 17. $4\overline{)26}$

Name _____

Practice
Chapters 1–12

Cumulative Review

(Chapter 8 Lesson 2) Complete the chart.

Shape	Number of Sides	Number of Corners
1. triangle		
2. circle		
3. rectangle		

(Chapter 9 Lesson 9) Find each product using mental math.

4. 42 × 5 = _____

5. 21 × 6 = _____

(Chapter 10 Lesson 12) Measure the length to the nearest $\frac{1}{4}$ inch.

(Chapter 11 Lesson 6) Use a ruler to measure the perimeter to the nearest centimeter.

6. _____

7. _____

(Chapter 12 Lesson 5) Write the temperature. Use °C or °F.

8.
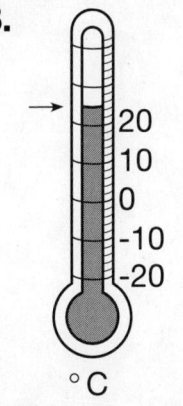
°C

_____

9.
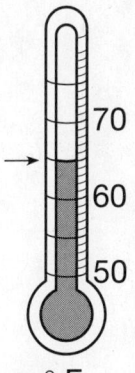
°F

_____

10.
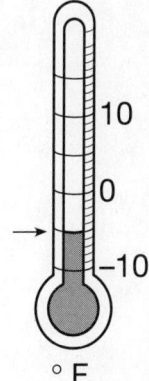
°F

_____

Use with page 517.

Name _____

Date _____ Score _____

Chapter 1 Test
Form **A**

Vocabulary: In 1–3, match each with its meaning.

1. key
2. pictograph
3. bar graph

a. a graph that uses bars to show data
b. part of a pictograph that tells what each symbol shows
c. a graph that uses pictures, or symbols, to show data

1. _____
2. _____
3. _____

In 4–5, use the pictograph.

4. What is the least popular sport?
   _____

5. How many students chose soccer?
   _____

Favorite Sports	
Tennis	☺☺
Soccer	☺☺☺
Basketball	☺☺☺☺
Football	☺☺☺

☺ = 2 votes

In 6–7, use the bar graph.

6. What subject has 20 votes?
   _____

7. How many more students prefer math than science?
   _____

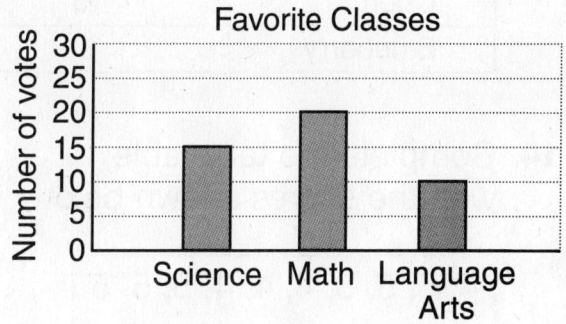

In 8–9, use the line graph.

8. How many books did Joe read in Week 3?
   _____

9. How many more books did Joe read in Week 3 than in Week 1?
   _____

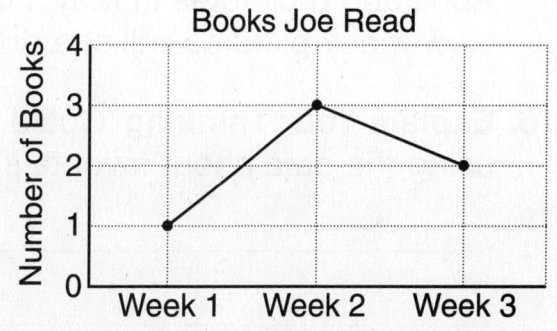

Chapter 1 Test Form A

Continued

Name _____

10. Write which operation you would use. Then solve. Kay has 4 oranges. She picks 3 more. How many does she have in all? _____

11. Complete the table. Then give its rule.

In	5	6	7	8	10
Out	1	2	3		

_____

In 12–13, use the data in the tables. Complete each graph.

12.

Favorite Season	
Season	Number
Spring	6
Summer	4
Fall	8
Winter	5

Favorite Season	
Spring	✳ ✳ ✳
Summer	✳ ✳
Fall	
Winter	

✳ = 2 votes

13.

Favorite Frozen Yogurt	
Flavor	Number
Vanilla	10
Chocolate	20
Cherry	15
Blueberry	5

14. Complete the tally table with the scores shown below.

4, 5, 5, 5, 4, 4, 4, 5, 5, 5

Scores	Tally	Number
4		
5		

15. Inga drew 2 pictures in March, 5 pictures in April, and 8 pictures in May. Find a pattern. How many pictures will she draw in June?

15. _____

16. Explain Your Thinking Could you draw a bar graph using the data about favorite seasons in Item 12? Explain.

_____

_____

2 Chapter 1 Test Form A

Name _____   **Chapter 2 Test**
Date _____ Score _____   Form **A**

Vocabulary: In 1–3, match each with its meaning.

1. place value
2. estimate
3. A.M.

a. times between midnight and noon
b. the value given to the place a digit has in a number
c. to find a number that is close to the exact number

1. _____
2. _____
3. _____

In 4–5, write each number in standard form.

4. 600 + 40 + 9

5. six thousand, two hundred forty-six

4. _____
5. _____

6. Write the word name for 607. _____

7. Write the word name for 5,210 _____

In 8–9, write each missing value.

8. 90 ones = ■ tens

9. ■ tens = 5 hundreds

8. _____
9. _____

In 10–11, write the value of each underlined digit.

10. 379,6<u>2</u>5

11. <u>9</u>34,271

10. _____
11. _____

12. Carmen wants to pack 45 books in boxes that hold 10 books or 1 book. How many ways can she pack the boxes?

12. _____

In 13–14, compare. Use <, >, or =.

13. 435 ● 921

14. 3,215 ● 2,513

13. _____
14. _____

15. Order 413, 431, and 341 from greatest to least.

15. _____

Chapter 2 Test Form A   Continued   3

Name _____

16. Round 87 to the nearest ten.   16. _____

17. Round 315 to the nearest ten.   17. _____

18. Round 245 to the nearest hundred.   18. _____

19. Round 552 to the nearest hundred.   19. _____

In 20–21, write each time in two ways.

20.   **21.**   20. _____

_____

21. _____

In 22–23, write each time in two ways. Write A.M. or P.M.

22.   **23.**   22. _____

_____

23. _____

_____

set dinner table   school starts

24. Chris cleaned for 2 hours and 5 minutes. He   24. _____
started at 9:00 A.M. What time did he finish?

25. LaRonda had dance class from 4:00 P.M.   25. _____
until 5:05 P.M. How long was the class?

26. What is the eighth month?   26. _____

27. Explain Your Thinking Which numbers round to 250
when rounded to the nearest ten? Which of these
numbers round to 200 when rounded to the nearest
hundred? Explain why your answers don't match.

_____

_____

_____

4 Chapter 2 Test Form A

Name _____

Date _____ Score _____

Chapter 3 Test
Form
A

Vocabulary: In 1–3, match each with its example.

1. sum
2. regroup
3. addend

a. a number that is added to find a sum
b. the number obtained when adding numbers
c. to name a number in a different way

1. _____
2. _____
3. _____

In 4, complete the number sentences.

4. $4 + 3 = \blacksquare$

$40 + \blacksquare = 70$

$\blacksquare + 300 = 700$

4. _____
_____
_____

In 5–6, find each sum. You may use a hundred chart to help.

5. $27 + 30$

6. $46 + 15$

5. _____
6. _____

In 7–8, find each missing number. You may use color cubes to help.

7. $14 + \blacksquare = 21$

8. $\blacksquare + 16 = 24$

7. _____
8. _____

In 9–12, find each sum. Estimate to check.

9. 57
   +25

10. 314
    +454

11. 3,518
    + 341

12. 17
     23
    +45

9. _____
10. _____
11. _____
12. _____

Chapter 3 Test Form A

Continued 5

Name _____

13. Guess and check to solve. Jan has 3 more red bows than green bows. She has 15 bows in all. How many green bows does she have?

13. _____

In 14–15, use mental math to find each sum.

14. 23 + 9

14. _____

15. 48 + 12

15. _____

In 16–17, write the total value.

16.

16. _____

17.

17. _____

18. Basil buys a fruit juice that costs $0.85. He pays with $5.00. Write the change in dollars and cents.

18. _____

In 19–20, add.

19. $3.71 + $1.25

19. _____

20. $1.37 + $2.61

20. _____

In 21–22, use rounding to estimate each sum.

21. 38 + 53

21. _____

22. 523 + 172

22. _____

In 23–24, use front-end estimation to estimate each sum.

23. 428 + 219

23. _____

24. 374 + 425

24. _____

25. Explain Your Thinking How much would it cost to buy 1 red pencil for $0.95, 1 black pen for $0.89, and 1 blue pen for $0.79? Explain whether you need an exact answer or an estimate.

_____

Name _____

Date _____ Score _____

Chapter 4 Test
Form **A**

In 1–2, write a number sentence for each. Then solve.

1. Carlos owns 5 baseballs and 2 mitts. How many more baseballs does Carlos own than mitts?

2. Sue made 4 soccer goals in her first game and 6 soccer goals in her second game. How many more goals did she make in her second game?

1. _____

2. _____

In 3–4, find each difference using mental math.

3. If $5 - 2 = 3$, then $50 - 20 = $ ■.

4. If $9 - 4 = 5$, then $900 - $ ■ $= 500$.

3. _____

4. _____

In 5–12, subtract. Check each answer.

5. 48
   −21

6. 34
   −18

7. $52 - 27$

8. $68 - 47$

9. 357
   − 23

10. 219
    −138

5. _____
6. _____
7. _____
8. _____
9. _____
10. _____

11. $483 - 298$

12. $725 - 367$

11. _____
12. _____

In 13–15, estimate each difference.

13. $35 - 21$

14. $562 - 221$

15. $\$4.89 - \$1.76$

13. _____
14. _____
15. _____

16. Regroup 1 ten for 10 ones: $78 = 6$ tens ■ ones. Write the missing number.

16. _____

Chapter 4 Test Form A

Continued **7**

Name _____

17. Regroup 1 hundred for 10 tens:
356 = ■ hundreds ■ tens 6 ones.
Write the missing numbers.

17. _____

In 18–19, subtract. Check each answer.

18. 207 − 64

18. _____

19. 404 − 38

19. _____

In 20–21, solve. Check each answer.

20. 3,786 − 1,252

20. _____

21. 5,703 − 1,538

21. _____

22. A paint brush costs $3. A set of paints costs $4. Elle bought two brushes and two sets of paints. How much more did she spend on paints than on brushes?

22. _____

In 23–24, write what number you would add to each in order to subtract mentally. Then subtract.

23. 37 − 19

23. _____

24. 64 − 27

24. _____

In 25–26, subtract.

25. $3.58 − $1.27

25. _____

26. $6.28 − $2.57

26. _____

27. Charon uses 3 drops of yellow paint for every 2 drops of blue paint. If she uses 9 drops of yellow, how many drops of blue will she use?

27. _____

28. Explain Your Thinking Use the digits 0, 2, 4, 5, 6, and 8 to write two money amounts that you can subtract by trading 1 dime for 10 pennies. Then solve.

_____

8 Chapter 4 Test Form A

Name _____
Date _____ Score _____

Chapter 5 Test Form A

Vocabulary: use 2 × 4 = 8 to answer 1–3.

1. Write the product.

2. Write the factors.

3. 8 is a multiple of ■.

1. _____
2. _____
3. _____

In 4–5, copy and complete.

4.
• •   • •   • •
• •   • •   • •
• •   • •   • •
• •   • •   • •

■ + ■ + ■ = ■   _____

■ groups of ■ equals ■.   _____

■ × ■ = ■   _____

5.
• •   • •   • •   • •
• •   • •   • •   • •

■ + ■ + ■ + ■ = ■   _____

■ groups of ■ equals ■.   _____

■ × ■ = ■   _____

6. Some camels have 2 humps. How many humps would 5 of these camels have? Write the multiplication sentence and give the answer.

6. _____

7. A fly has 6 legs. How many legs would 3 flies have? You may use counters to solve.

7. _____

8. Some spiders have 4 eyes. How many eyes would 5 spiders have? You may use counters to help.

8. _____

Chapter 5 Test Form A   *Continued*

Name _____

In 9–32, find each product.

9. 2
   $\underline{\times 2}$

10. 2
    $\underline{\times 3}$

11. 4
    $\underline{\times 2}$

12. 2
    $\underline{\times 7}$

13. 5
    $\underline{\times 3}$

14. 4
    $\underline{\times 5}$

15. 7
    $\underline{\times 5}$

16. 5
    $\underline{\times 8}$

17. 4
    $\underline{\times 9}$

18. 9
    $\underline{\times 6}$

19. 7
    $\underline{\times 9}$

20. 9
    $\underline{\times 9}$

21. 8
    $\underline{\times 1}$

22. 1
    $\underline{\times 6}$

23. 0
    $\underline{\times 4}$

24. 3
    $\underline{\times 0}$

25. 2×8 _____

26. 5×6 _____

27. 9×3 _____

28. 1×2 _____

29. 0×4 _____

30. 2×6 _____

31. 1×7 _____

32. 9×7 _____

33. There are 5 sticks of gum in a package. Each package costs $0.50. How many sticks of gum are in 3 packages?

    33. _____

34. **Explain Your Thinking** Manford is making a necklace that will have 9 beads. Beads 1 and 9 will have the same color, beads 2 and 8 will have the same color, and so on. Explain what strategy you might use to find the number of different colors needed. Then give the answer.

_____

_____

_____

_____

Name _____   **Chapter 6 Test**
Date _____ Score _____   Form
                                                   A

Vocabulary: In 1–3, match each with its meaning.

1. square number   a. the product of a given whole   1. _____
                        number and any other whole
                        number

2. grouping   2. _____
                     b. the product when both factors
                        are the same

3. multiple   c. when you multiply, you can   3. _____
                        group factors in any order and
                        the product will be the same

In 4–19, find each product.

| 4.   3 | 5.   6 | 6.   4 | 7.   9 |
| × 5 | × 3 | × 2 | × 4 |

| 8.   6 | 9.   9 | 10. 7 | 11. 5 |
| × 5 | × 6 | × 3 | × 7 |

12. 4 × 8   13. 3 × 8   14. 7 × 6   15. 6 × 2

16. 9 × 7   17. 7 × 8   18. 6 × 8   19. 8 × 8

20. Nina bought 6 packages of butter. Each   20. _____
    package contains 4 sticks. How many
    sticks of butter did Nina buy?

21. A group of students were taking a field trip. 21. _____
    They traveled in 7 vans with 5 students
    riding in each van. How many students
    were going on the trip?

Chapter 6 Test Form A   Continued 11

Name _____

In 22–24, write *true* or *false*. You may use a hundred chart to help.

22. 21 is a multiple of 3. 22. _____

23. 35 is a multiple of 3. 23. _____

24. 36 is a multiple of 6. 24. _____

In 25–27, continue each pattern.

25. 40, 50, 60, ■, ■, ■ 25. _____

26. 77, 66, 55, ■, ■, ■ 26. _____

27. 36, 48, 60, ■, ■, ■ 27. _____

In 28–31, find each product.

28. 2 × 3 × 4 28. _____

29. (3 × 2) × 8 29. _____

30. 1 × (4 × 7) 30. _____

31. 3 × (1 × 6) 31. _____

32. Tim has 4 board games. Each game can have 4 players. Will Tim have enough games so that he and 23 friends can play at one time? Explain.

_____

33. Juanita is mixing pitchers of lemonade for the 29 students in her class. One pitcher will serve 4 students. How many pitchers does she need to make? 33. _____

34. Explain Your Thinking Explain how you can use the product of 4 × 3 to find 8 × 3. Then give the product.

_____

_____

_____

Name _____
Date _____ Score _____

Chapter 7 Test Form A

Vocabulary: In 1–4, match each with its meaning.

1. divisor
2. quotient
3. odd number
4. even number

a. a whole number that has 0, 2, 4, 6 or 8 in the ones place

b. the number by which a dividend is divided

c. the answer to a division problem

d. a whole number that has 1, 3, 5, 7, or 9 in the ones place

1. _____
2. _____
3. _____
4. _____

5. Complete the division sentence.

   6 ÷ 2 = ■

5. _____

6. 8 dogs
   2 in each pen
   How many pens?

6. _____

In 7–9, complete.

7. 8 × ☐ = 24
   24 ÷ ☐ = 8

8. 7 × ☐ = 56
   56 ÷ 7 = ☐

9. ☐ × 7 = 35
   35 ÷ ☐ = 7

In 10–21, find each quotient.

10. 12 ÷ 2
11. 25 ÷ 5
12. 5 ÷ 1
13. 28 ÷ 4

14. 2)‾16‾
15. 3)‾21‾
16. 6)‾0‾
17. 5)‾40‾

18. 54 ÷ 6
19. 64 ÷ 8
20. 49 ÷ 7
21. 72 ÷ 9

Chapter 7 Test Form A   Continued

Name _____

22. Ruby has 42 dollar bills. She gave 7 dollar bills to each of her nieces. How many nieces does she have?

22. _____

23. Victor shared 28 stickers equally with 3 friends. How many stickers did each person get? (Remember that Victor will have the same number of stickers as each of his friends.)

23. _____

In 24–25, write which operation you would use to solve the problem. Then solve.

24. A loaf of nut bread has 18 slices. If a serving is 3 slices, how many servings are there?

_____

25. Arimoto bought 9 tickets to the choir recital. Each ticket cost $5. How much money did he spend?

_____

26. The band has 20 members that will march in a parade. They will march in equal rows. What are all the ways the leader can arrange them?

_____

_____

27. Box A has 10 cubes inside. Box B has 4 cubes inside. How many cubes are inside Box C?

27. _____

28. Write the next 4 odd numbers after 25.

28. _____

29. Write the next 4 even numbers after 10.

29. _____

30. Explain Your Thinking Arthur has 3 groups of 5 plants. Which operations could you use to find how many plants he has in all? Explain.

_____

_____

14 Chapter 7 Test Form A

Name _____

Date _____ Score _____

Chapter 8 Test
Form **A**

Vocabulary: In 1–4, match each with its example.

1.
2.
3.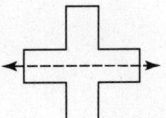
4.

____ ____ ____ ____

a. line of symmetry	**b.** line
c. cylinder	**d.** right angle

In 5–7, name the solid figure or shape that each object looks like.

5.
6.
7.

____ ____ ____

8. Are these lines parallel or intersecting?  ____

9. Is this angle a right angle, less than a right angle, or greater than a right angle? 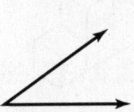 ____

In 10–12, write congruent or not congruent for each.

10.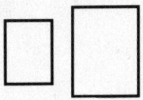
11.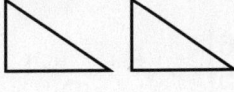
12.

____ ____ ____

In 13–15, write slide, flip, or turn.

13.
14.
15.

____ ____ ____

Chapter 8 Test Form A   Continued 15

Name _____

In 16–18, is each a line of symmetry? Write *yes* or *no*.

16.

17.

18.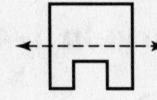

_____   _____   _____

19. How many squares are in this design?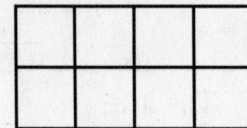

19. _____

In 20–21, find the perimeter and the area of each figure.

20.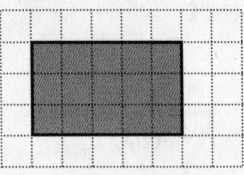

Perimeter _____

Area _____

21.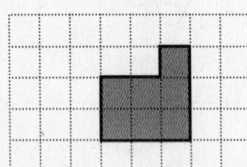

Perimeter _____

Area _____

In 22–24, find the volume of each.

22.    23. 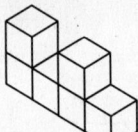   24.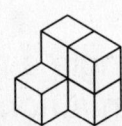

_____   _____   _____

In 25–26, write the ordered pair that locates each letter.

25. A _____

26. B _____

27. Which letter is located at (2, 5)? _____

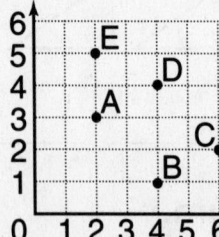

28. **Explain Your Thinking** Use 4 line segments to draw a polygon that has 4 right angles.

16 Chapter 8 Test Form A

Name _____   **Chapter 9 Test**
Date _____ Score _____   Form **A**

In 1–2, complete. You may use place-value blocks.

1. 9 × 1 ten = ■ tens _____
   9 × 10 = ■ _____

2. 6 × 7 tens = ■ tens _____
   6 × 70 = ■ _____

In 3–4, complete.

3. 7 × 5 = ■ _____
   7 × 50 = ■ _____
   7 × 500 = ■ _____

4. 3 × 8 = ■ _____
   3 × 80 = ■ _____
   3 × 800 = ■ _____

In 5–7, estimate each product.

5. 4 × 37   5. _____
6. 6 × 92   6. _____
7. 7 × 523   7. _____

In 8–9, find each product. You may use place value blocks to help.

8. 3 × 16   8. _____

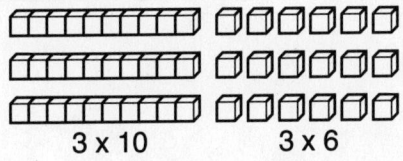
3 x 10   3 x 6

9. 2 × 21   9. _____

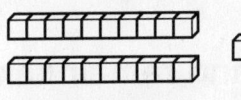
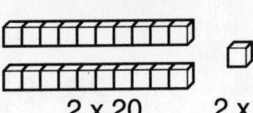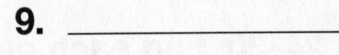
2 x 20   2 x 1

In 10–17, find each product.

10. 46 × 5   10. _____

11. 28 × 6   11. _____

12.   1 3   13.   2 8   12. _____
    × 9   × 7   13. _____

14.   2 4 7   15.   6 0 2   14. _____
    ×   5   ×   7   15. _____

Chapter 9 Test Form A   Continued 17

Name _____

16. $3.26
    ×   5

17. $4.78
    ×   4

16. _____

17. _____

In 18–19, find each product using mental math.

18. 37 × 5

19. 18 × 7

18. _____

19. _____

In 20, complete the table to solve.

20. At the end of the first week, Clyde mowed 9 lawns. After the second week, he had mowed 18 lawns. If the pattern continues, how many weeks will it take him to mow 36 lawns?

20. _____

Week	1	2	3	4	5
Lawns	9	18			

In 21–23, estimate each quotient.

21. 64 ÷ 7

22. 18 ÷ 5

23. 50 ÷ 8

21. _____

22. _____

23. _____

In 24–30, find each quotient and remainder.

24. 6)$\overline{32}$ 25. 5)$\overline{19}$ 26. 9)$\overline{55}$

27. 22 ÷ 3

28. 15 ÷ 4

29. 74 ÷ 8

27. _____

28. _____

29. _____

30. **Explain Your Thinking** How can you use patterns to find each quotient? Find the quotients.

27 ÷ 3 = ■
270 ÷ 3 = ■
2,700 ÷ 3 = ■

_____

_____

Chapter 9 Test Form A

Name _____

Date _____ Score _____

Chapter 10 Test
Form **A**

Vocabulary: In 1–3, match each with its meaning.

1. unit fraction
2. fraction
3. equivalent fractions

a. fractions that name the same amount
b. a fraction with a numerator of 1
c. a comparison of equal parts to a whole

1. _____
2. _____
3. _____

In 4–5, write the equal parts of each whole.

4.
5.

4. _____
5. _____

In 6–7, write the fraction of each figure that is shaded.

6.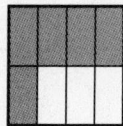
7.

6. _____
7. _____

In 8–9, are the fractions equivalent or not equivalent?

8.
9.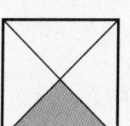

8. _____
9. _____

In 10–11, compare. Write <, >, or =.

10.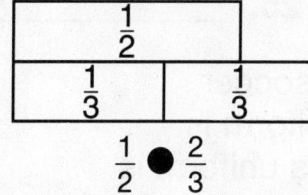
11.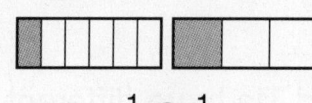

10. _____
11. _____

In 12–13, estimate the amount that is shaded.

12.
13.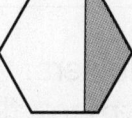

12. _____
13. _____

In 14–15, solve. You may draw a picture to help.

14. Find $\frac{1}{4}$ of 20.

15. Find $\frac{1}{5}$ of 15.

14. _____
15. _____

Chapter 10 Test Form A
Continued 19

Name _____

In 16–17, write a mixed number for each picture.

16. 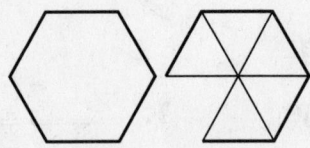   17.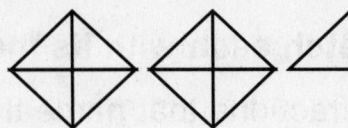

16. _____

17. _____

18. Find the difference. $\frac{5}{8} - \frac{3}{8}$

18. _____

19. Find the sum. $\frac{3}{10} + \frac{4}{10}$

19. _____

20. Measure the glue stick to the nearest inch.

20. _____

21. Measure the binder clip to the nearest $\frac{1}{2}$ inch.

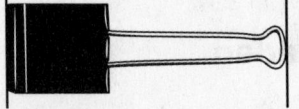

21. _____

22. Measure the pen cap to the nearest $\frac{1}{4}$ inch.

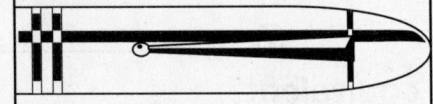

22. _____

23. Write 1 foot 6 inches in inches.

23. _____

In 24–25, compare. Write <, >, or =.

24. 3 yards ● 10 feet

24. _____

25. 72 inches ● 2 yards

25. _____

26. Shane, Jorie, Hoy, and Tia have different color soccer uniforms: white, yellow, blue, and red. Hoy's uniform is white. Jorie's uniform matches her red hair. Tia's uniform is the color of the sky. What color is each person's uniform?

_____

27. **Explain Your Thinking** Draw 6 flowers. Color some of them. Write a fraction that names how many flowers are colored. Explain what the numerator and denominator mean.

_____

_____

Chapter 10 Test Form A

Name _____   Chapter 11 Test
Date _____ Score _____   Form A

Vocabulary: In 1–4 match each with its meaning.

1. decimal point   a. a metric unit of measure equal to 1,000 meters   1. _____

2. centimeter   b. a standard unit used to measure length in the metric system   2. _____

3. meter   c. symbol used to separate ones from tenths in a decimal   3. _____

4. kilometer   d. a metric unit of measure equal to 100 centimeters   4. _____

In 5–6, write the fraction and the decimal to name each shaded part.

5. 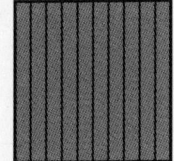   6.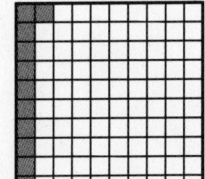

5. _____

6. _____

In 7–12, write each as a decimal.

7. $\frac{6}{10}$

8. $3\frac{8}{10}$

9. $5\frac{35}{100}$

10. four hundredths

11. two and fifty-two hundredths

12. one tenth

7. _____
8. _____
9. _____
10. _____
11. _____
12. _____

In 13–16, find each sum or difference.

13. 0.8
    + 0.4

14. 1.4
    + 2.9

15. 4.5
    − 1.3

16. 6.1
    − 3.8

13. _____
14. _____
15. _____
16. _____

Chapter 11 Test Form A   Continued

Name _____

In 17–20, write each as a money amount.

17. $\frac{34}{100}$ of $1.00   17. _____

18. $2\frac{50}{100}$ of $1.00   18. _____

19. eight cents   19. _____

20. one dollar and twenty-seven cents   20. _____

In 21–23, match each with its estimate.

21. length of a marker   a. 2 cm   21. _____

22. length of a river   b. 1 dm   22. _____

23. width of the face of a watch   c. 20 km   23. _____

In 24–26, write whether you would measure each in cm, m, or km.

24. distance of a bike ride   24. _____

25. length of the soccer field   25. _____

26. height of a small dog   26. _____

27. Suppose you get on an elevator on the third floor. The elevator goes up 2 floors, then up 5 more floors. It goes down 3 floors, and then up 4 floors. What floor is the elevator at now?   27. _____

28. There are 33 people on a tram. At the first stop, 2 more people get on and 4 get off. At the next stop, 8 people get off and 5 get on. At the next stop, 10 get off and 2 get on. How many people are on the tram now?   28. _____

29. **Explain Your Thinking** Diane shaded 4 rows of a hundredths square. Write a decimal to name the shaded part. Explain. You may use this hundredths grid to help.

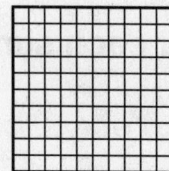

_____

_____

22 Chapter 11 Test Form A

Name _____

Date _____ Score _____

Chapter 12 Test
Form
A

Vocabulary: In 1–2, write true or false.

1. Capacity is the amount an object weighs.

2. Predictions are a guess about what will happen.

1. _____

2. _____

In 3–10, write the best estimate for each.

3.
1 cup
1 quart
1 gallon

4.
1 cup
1 quart
1 gallon

3. _____

4. _____

5.
59 mL
59 L

6.
8 mL
8 L

5. _____

6. _____

7.
5 oz
5 lb

8.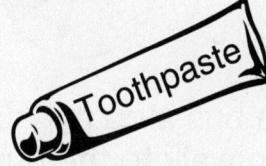
6 oz
6 lb

7. _____

8. _____

9.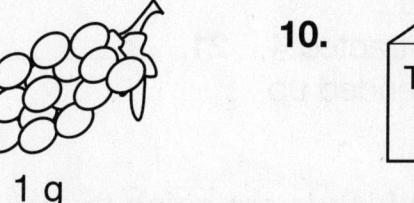
1 g
1 kg

10.
6 g
6 kg

9. _____

10. _____

In 11–12, write each temperature using °F.

11.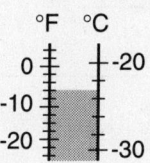

12.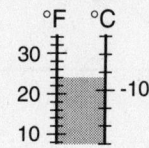

11. _____

12. _____

Chapter 12 Test Form A   Continued 23

Name _____

In 13–14, decide whether each is likely or unlikely.

13. You will drive a car tomorrow. 13. _____

14. Someone in your class is 9 years old. 14. _____

In 15–16, suppose you put these cubes in a bag. Predict which color you are more likely to pull out.

15. 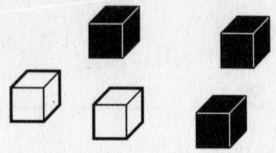   16.

15. _____

16. _____

17. Copy and complete.   White: ■ out of 6 or $\frac{\blacksquare}{6}$ 17. _____

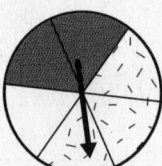

Gray: ■ out of 6 or $\frac{\blacksquare}{6}$ _____

Dotted: ■ out of 6 or $\frac{\blacksquare}{6}$ _____

In 18–19, write whether each spinner is fair or unfair.

18. 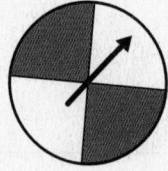   19.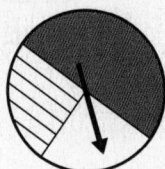

18. _____

19. _____

20. Anne needs to be at the bus stop by 7:35 A.M. It takes her 5 minutes to walk to the bus stop and 45 minutes to get ready. At what time must she get up?   20. _____

21. Janet picked a number. Then she subtracted 4, added 6, and subtracted 10. If Janet ended up with 50, what number did she pick?   21. _____

22. **Explain Your Thinking** Lionel and 2 friends are going to camp out in Lionel's back yard. Lionel thinks that each of the three boys will drink 1,000 mL of sports drink. He buys one 2-L bottle. Did he buy enough? Explain.

_____

Name _____

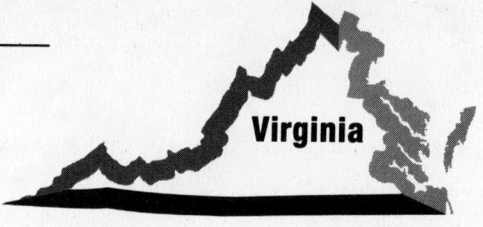

Related Facts: Addition and Subtraction

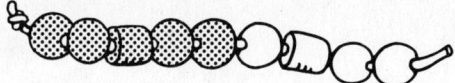

5 + 4 = 9 and 9 − 4 = 5 are **related facts.**

They both have the same numbers.

1. Write the pair of related facts shown by the pictures.

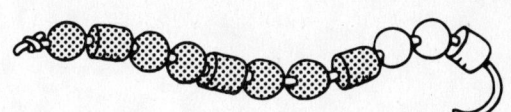 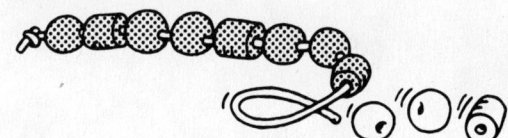

_____   _____

Use each addition fact to complete the subtraction fact.

2. 5 + 6 = 11   **3.** 4 + 8 = 12   **4.** 6 + 7 = 13

　　11 − 6 = ____　　　　12 − 8 = ____　　　　13 − 7 = ____

5. 9 + 5 = 14   **6.** 9 + 8 = 17   **7.** 7 + 9 = 16

　　14 − 5 = ____　　　　17 − 8 = ____　　　　16 − 9 = ____

Subtract. Then write a related addition fact.

8. 14 − 8 = ____   **9.** 15 − 8 = ____   **10.** 18 − 9 = ____

_____   _____   _____

11. 10 − 7 = ____   **12.** 12 − 5 = ____   **13.** 13 − 8 = ____

_____   _____   _____

Virginia Mathematics Standards of Learning: (3.4) The student will recognize and use the inverse relationship between addition/subtraction and multiplication/division to complete basic facts sentences. Students will use these relationships to solve problems such as 5 + 3 = 8 and 8 − 3 = ____.

Use before Lesson 3-3.

SOL Lesson **1**

Name _____

Related Facts: Multiplication and Division

Virginia

Rudy's toy cars are displayed on 3 shelves, with 8 cars on each shelf.

$3 \times 8 = 24$
$24 \div 8 = 3$

$3 \times 8 = 24$ and $24 \div 8 = 3$ are **related facts**.

They both have the same numbers.

1. Write the pair of related facts shown by the picture.

____ × ____ = ____

____ ÷ ____ = ____

Use each multiplication fact to complete the division fact.

2. $9 \times 7 = 63$ **3.** $4 \times 8 = 32$ **4.** $9 \times 2 = 18$

$63 \div 7 =$ ____ $32 \div 8 =$ ____ $18 \div 2 =$ ____

5. $5 \times 8 = 40$ **6.** $7 \times 8 = 56$ **7.** $7 \times 3 = 21$

$40 \div 8 =$ ____ $56 \div 8 =$ ____ $21 \div 3 =$ ____

Divide. Then write a related multiplication fact.

8. $14 \div 7 =$ ____   **9.** $15 \div 3 =$ ____   **10.** $36 \div 9 =$ ____

_____   _____   _____

11. $16 \div 2 =$ ____   **12.** $45 \div 5 =$ ____   **13.** $42 \div 6 =$ ____

_____   _____   _____

Virginia Mathematics Standards of Learning: (3.4) Recognize and use the inverse relationship between addition/subtraction and multiplication/division to complete basic facts sentences.

Use before Lesson 7-4.

Name _____

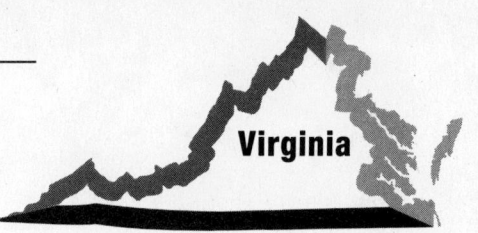

Create and Solve Problems Involving Multiplication

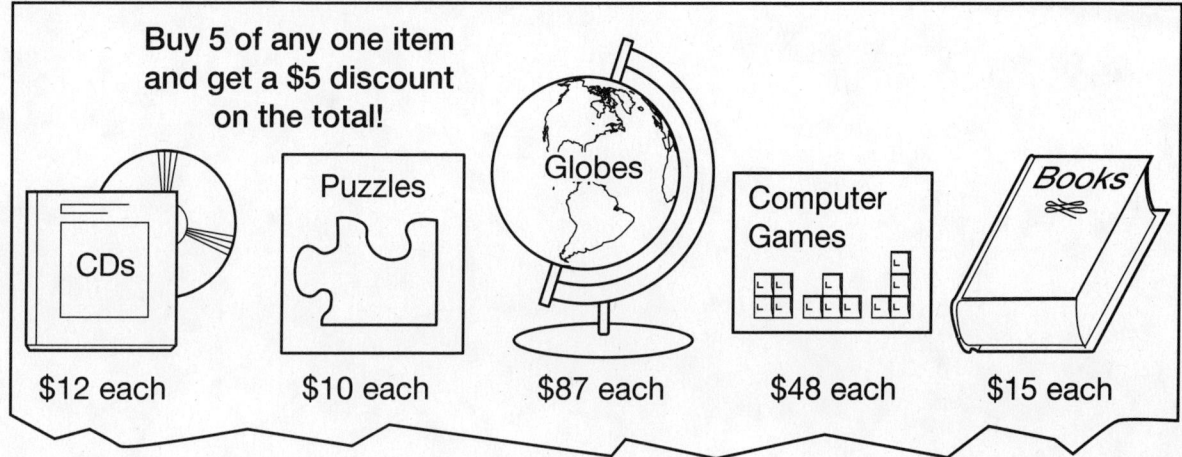

The Wildwood School Parents' Club is deciding which materials to buy for the school library and resource center. Some of the catalog items they can choose are pictured above with their prices. The club will not buy more than 5 of any one item. They have $500 to spend.

Create a problem about buying 5 of any one item.

Sample Problem: The club chose 5 CDs at $12 each and got the $5 discount. How much did they pay for the CDs?

$$5 \times 12 = 60 \qquad 60 - 5 = 55$$

The cost of 5 CDs was $55.

Using the data above, create a problem about each of the following. Then solve the problem.

1. Buying 4 of one item

2. Buying 2 of one item and 5 of another item

3. Buying 5 each of three different items

4. Finding how much money will be left after buying 3 each of four different items

5. Comparing costs: 2 of one item compared to 3 of a less expensive item

---

Virginia Mathematics Standards of Learning: (3.10) Create and solve problems that involve multiplication of two whole numbers, one factor 99 or less and the second factor 5 or less.

Use after Lesson 9-6.   SOL Lesson **3**